AS A MAN THINKETH…
In His Heart

A Novel

by

James Michael Pratt

A novel inspired by the 1902 bestselling timeless classic
As A Man Thinketh by James Allen

❧❧

"As a man thinketh, in his heart, so is he."
—*Proverbs of Solomon*

Cover design and content layout by Evan Frederickson

Photo: "View of Ilfracome harbour, town and Torrs, 1890's" Ilfracombe Museum

Library of Congress Cataloging-in-Publication Data is available from the Library of Congress
Catalogue Data Pending
ISBN 0-9815596-1-1
HEARTLAND BOOKS
PowerThink Publishing
2020 Fieldstone Pkwy Ste. 900
Franklin, TN. 37069
Visit us at www.powerthink.com

Printed in the United States of America
10 9 8 7 6 5 4 3 2 1

For Jeanne who believes!

❧

Amor est vitae essentia

Ilfracombe, England 1900

৯৩ৎ৫

"The most beautiful thing we can experience is mysterious.
It is the source of all art and success."
-Albert Einstein

AUTHOR'S FORWARD

The success of a creative tale is measured by a reader's enjoyment found in it. As a reading journey goes, we find places our feet may not have traveled, but our hearts and minds surely have. After all, what matters is what one *believes*.

In this story some personal author history blended with literary license might seem to conspire with the phrase, "Stranger than fiction." For the benefit of the reader I shall asterisk (*) where those sometimes humorous or poignant stretches of the imagination meet true events from my life, and in the development of this story.

These passages shall then be offered in detail at an "online" website dedicated to answering reader inquiries regarding factual versions of the story–building events in question.

Beware. Unusual and entertaining things may happen in cyberspace; the same kinds of things that perhaps you would have found written on a piece of paper which floated your way, or in a book that just happened to open to the right page when you least expected it – but with a message meant just for you.

I promise you this: You will find something custom-made for you as you lose yourself in any story where love, mystery, and timeless truths collide. Whatever your reason for trusting this tale, I am honored you are with me on a trip of discovery.

Though my path to Ilfracombe was unwittingly begun at age 19,* I recently found unexpected truth in a magical guided tour to a land, a heart, and a mind I could have never known until, *As a Man Thinketh...In His Heart*. I now share it with you.

PROLOGUE

"James, lie down – please!" his wife gently scolded. "You'll catch your death of cold," she admonished. She had brought a cot into the study so he could easily rest near his beloved books and writing table.

She was over forty but God had been kind to her and age did not seem to affect the outward softness or beauty. She easily passed for someone young enough to be an older sister to their recently deceased college-educated godchild.

He shook his head, waving her off with his left hand as his right furiously penned the final words to ACT I. "I mustn't let them down," he wheezed. *Once I finish this tale I can continue writing my treatise on the voice of the Intuitive heart,* he posed silently.

He coughed heavily. She set the tea before him on the writing desk and placed her arm around him. "My darling James…" she sighed, pulling the shawl tightly around his neck and shoulders.

James appeared twenty years more than his chronological age due to this nagging illness which had intensified since last winter. He had fought her efforts to seek medical help through the spring and summer months and his cough had worsened along with weakening his general strength.

She brought her face down to his and said, "I fear for you, my love! I have sent for Doctor Brown. Now you must complete your writing later! Please James… You worry me, darling."

He gazed up to see an expression of helplessness in her eyes. He placed his pen on his writing tablet and sipped from the tea she had placed before him. It soothed his throat enough for him to say, as he nodded in agreement, "Later… You are quite right. Always…" he weakly stated. "Always…"

He reached up, as if to lovingly touch her ever youthful, kind, but angelic cherub features. "Lily, *my LOVE*…" he let out with great effort.

"James!" she shouted, as he collapsed to the floor. She knelt before her husband of two decades. His eyes had rolled back into his head and yet he was alive, wheezing, struggling for breath with the severe chest ailment.

"Your head! James, you are burning with fever!"

A slight woman, but strong, she struggled to raise him from the floor and place him into the bed. "Singh!" she called. "Oh dear… God! Singh, please help me!"

Her cry alerted the house guest and successful businessman from London. A faithful friend of his philosophy and her cousin through marriage, he had waited with courtesy outside the study door.

The man looked at his friend. "So pale," he said as he rushed to scoop James up into his strong arms. "You will be needing to get Doctor Brown! Go!" he admonished Lily. "I will care for James! Go!"

The stricken man coughed heavily as he tried to focus on the voice he had come to know through so much discussion regarding life, faith, death, and *meaning*. "Singh…" he weakly offered.

"Master James, drink," Singh offered as he tipped the weakened man's head back, pouring the remainder of the soothing chrysanthemum tea into parched lips. Sadness showed from the stoic Sikh from Punjab; it showed in eyes which had learned to look beyond emotions.

"The medal…" he coughed. "Minted, yes?"

"One thousand copper medallions, Master. One for each printed book."

"I am no Master. You are…" he said, weakly pointing.

"We shall make them available to friends, book sellers, publishers… As soon as you regain your strength and finish your edit." Singh undid the coin purse hanging from his belt and took one specially minted medallion from the small bag.

He read the Latin inscriptions. On top of one side was the word "Thought." Engraved on the bottom was "EX NIHILO NIHIL FIT." On the flip side another Latin axiom was engraved on the upper edge; "EX TEMPORE," with "Power" meticulously minted into the soft metal on the bottom rim of the copper coin.

Both sides carried the Latin word "EX ANIMO," center-etched with MCMXII beneath a silhouette form of a man in thought. Rays of light in the background illuminated the male profile as an artist might portray such strands of luminescence coming forth from the bright noon day sun.

He nodded approvingly. "Dear friend. I…" James struggled as he slid into the dark sleep of the seriously ill. His breathing eased along with the distressed and tortured appearance of an aged man's face giving way to peace. A faint smile seemed to purse his lips.

"Rest, Master. Rest…" The Sikh had placed James upon the cot and now pulled the blanket up tight around the shoulders of a skeletal outer shell.

Singh had fought in India for the King and Crown. He had seen men die in battle but just as often from infectious disease. He wished to rescue his mentor of the thinking arts but the only words coming to his mind now were prayer-like as he knelt beside the stricken man's frail body.

Be at peace and God go before you. The Brotherhood of Righteousness shall stand as witness to your integrity forever. Your faithful friend shall not forget nor cease to serve. Rest, Master James.

ACT I

COGNITO ERGO SUM

1
MR. TOAD'S WILD RIDE

Present Day – Montana Hotel London.

Journal Entry October Week 1

I should have gone to Disneyland. I had sent my wife west to her brother's home in California; a vacation to the beach and of course to be with family at her favorite theme park, Disneyland. I was a kid once. Wonder what happened. I never could unwind as easily as my wife. She is on "kid auto-pilot" 24/7. I traveled east, across the "pond" as the Brits like to say, to begin the search for the mysterious author and the unfinished story that has captivated me for over one year now.

***

I put the pen down, threw myself on to a cushioned king size bed, stretched, and yawned. "*Disneyland,*" I allowed to no one else in the room. It was mid-day, and after figuring out how to connect from Heathrow on the underground "Circle Line," I had just checked in. Jet lag and an inordinate amount of stress was taking its toll

I hadn't slept much in the past two days and thought I should journal the unusual happenings while they were fresh in my mind. *I'll get back to it in a minute*, I thought. Placing hands behind my head, my eyes gazed into the smooth white ceiling of the tiny but tidy hotel room.

After a tenuous two days of everything from giving lectures on a topic that ultimately brought me here, to slaying three proverbial dragons of the traveling nightmare sort, I knew that if I had been with Jeanne at Southern California's Disneyland, and we had just finished the MR. TOAD'S WILD RIDE, it would have at least ended with, "Let's do that again!"

Three airports, forty-eight hours, and what should be an illegal amount of insanity, nearly had me turn back at each attempt to continue on my journey across the Atlantic. *Yet*, I mused, *for all the opposition I faced in getting here, there have been equally compelling coincidences pushing me on.*

My sense of mission and "a call" to partner with the eloquent and mysterious writer of yesteryear had become as real to me as if I had been officially sent a personally signed invitation to travel to England and participate in finishing his tale.

And that is what this is really about, I considered. I reminded myself to get up from the soft comfort of this luxury hotel's over-sized poster bed and recall that story now – in journal form – before the "mind over mattress" effort failed.

My body simply would not obey my sleep-deprived mind. I studied the scenes developing for me on the overhead ceiling; a screen to project my thoughts on to. My mind easily faded now – to when it began so innocently one year ago – this search for a story and its unknown English author.

2

Mystery

Who doesn't like a good mystery replete with coded words, clues, and a sense of adventure? I silently posed as slumber-land began to invade my otherwise overly-active mind. *How does one know what lies beyond the clues, unless risks are taken? That is why I am here, isn't it?* I questioned. *Where did this journey begin?* I noiselessly probed. *Ah yes… A phone call and…*

Last Year

"Hi, Maryann. What's new?"

"Jim, an agent wants to chat with you about that epic period-piece; the love saga you shared with me… It begins with a British Navy officer, a romance, tragedy…"

"The Revolutionary War period– Right?"

"That's the one. You know the elements… history, love, war; the stuff you do so well. I think the timing works for a potential film script/book deal," she said.

"A little 'through-line moral' doesn't hurt, does it?"

"Remember Jim, less is more in Hollywood and New York."

"Subtlety."

"That's what they want. Let the action do the talking."

"Got it."

"That sample content you based your story outline on… You finally find the original source?"

"Working on it."

"Is it copyrighted?"

"I feel fairly confident that this is turn-of-the-twentieth century writing. Meaning, if it is over sixty years-old, the phantom writer's material should be legally available in the 'public domain.'"

"I'm still not clear how you found it once but now can't find the original source. Review that for me."

"Sure, Maryann. It was last year. I was doing an Internet search looking for something Shakespeare reportedly said. I was trying to verify a quote for use in one of my stories in progress. Somehow, I came across this storyline by the unknown writer, copied the content on to a separate Word doc, and printed it off. I just assumed the author's name printed out somewhere on the document."

"Hum. Well, what about the website you got it from?"

"I've been looking. I thought I saved the website in a folder, but apparently not."

"Well, good luck on that."

"I'm going to hire a computer search expert soon. We'll find the source. Not to worry."

"When can I see some sample chapters?"

"If I can't nail down the author's name this month, I'll come up with an original period piece myself. As to sample chapters; middle of next month okay? I want to check this out, polish it, and then deliver my best."

"Sounds great. Let's keep them hooked. Talk soon."

"Thanks, Maryann. Love all you do. Bye."

I hung up the rotary dial phone, seated next to the circa 1910 Olympia typewriter. The phone sat upon a pre-World War I roll-top desk originally built in England. The small desk, upon which both ancient pieces of office equipment sit, is special to me. I call it my "time machine," and often spend reading and story development time there.

"Who sat here before me? What did they write?" I asked quietly as my hand caressed the well-crafted walnut taken from some English estate. I paused in mental reverie at the gouge on top wondering how it was caused, before moving on to the task assigned to me by Maryann.

According to its history, the desk was custom-made for a turn-of-the-century account-ant in London somewhere, and then according to the auction house where I purchased it, the antique roll-top with a stack of side drawers was brought to Virginia, along with the Olympia typewriter, by a returning American Army doctor just after World War I, in 1919. I like to imagine it hides secrets absorbed into its desk-top from a thousand works of correspondence, ledger books, and conversations; the stuff common to early everyday 1900 English life.

To me these aged office items spanning over one hundred years of time, sit in mute testimony to the action once performed by men and women who lived their lives out around them – very much a real stage of life filled with hopes, dreams, needs, and belief that their world could never *really* end for them.

These remainders from historic days past are also subtle reminders that I too shall pass on from a scene of action to become as their prior owners are now – just voices of gentle ghosts whispering what seventeenth century Christian poet John Donne declared. I had memorized the well-known phrase, from which Ernest Hemingway created a book title. I whispered it now to test that memory.

No man is an island, I began. *Entire of itself; every man is a piece of the continent, a part of the main. If a clod be washed away by the sea, Europe is the less... Any man's death diminishes me, because I am involved in mankind; and therefore never send to know for whom the bell tolls; it tolls for thee.*

For some reason, which I couldn't quite define, the probable deceased author's bell seemed to only ring louder for me as I continued this search.

I was in need of getting back to Maryann "ASAP" on the use of the story in question. Finally rousing my senses and recalling the task at hand, I began to research. I didn't have the entire website name, but did have this much to go on: The words "power" and "think" behind the customary Internet address starting with: "http://..." That was it. Nothing more.*

I had no idea which computer folder I had saved this information in, or whether I simply printed the unknown author's content directly from the website in question when I first stumbled upon the English writer's story last year. Starting with the printed information, I looked under every computer desktop file I could for the mystery document which appeared out of cyberspace one year ago. "*Hampton of Devon* where are you?" I asked, in reference to the name of the main character.

This short piece of literary fiction, without an author identity, really had me stumped. How I could have found such an intriguing piece of classic Victorian handwritten prose and not filed the original copy and Internet source to my main "Book Ideas" folder, was a mystery. I'm never that careless with promising material.

In the unknown writer's own cursive he had referred to playwright William Shakespeare. "That's it!" I proudly announced to my empty home office. I quickly did a computer file search for "Bard." Nearly a year after having apparently saved it, an obscure file appeared on my computer screen titled, "BARD OF THE THEMES."

"Yeah!" I congratulated myself. "Now just follow the website links..."

Internet search capabilities are a writer's dream come true. Too many benefits to list, I was aware that this search to connect the material I had in my hand with an anonymous author was probably just a few key strokes away. I could then assure Maryann that I had a usable piece, and if the material proved to be copyrighted after all, I could simply thank the author for the inspiration I had received and move on with my own creatively written period-piece.

As often seemed the case, this content seemed to come forth at the precise time I required for pushing a story along which agent, manager, or others who wanted to see new material. I'm not sure what magic is at play for the writer when this occurs, but it happens with frequency.

What might seem strangely other-worldly to observers just becomes accepted to the composers of song and the written word. We "hear voices" and, borrowing a line from Shymalan's movie *Sixth Sense,* "see dead people." I can only describe this phenomenon as if friendly voices softly whisper... so soft it takes total "zoning out" from the present moment to hear them and obey. "Shrinks" call this phenomena psychosis. Writers and artists call it inspiration.

3
"Back Story"

As in all good stories, this tale has its own "back story." It's something every character and story has in common – those "set up" scenes and elements which cause the story a birth and which gives the character his depth and motivation in the first place.

The *back story* of my life, prior to becoming a writer of some reputation in my early forties, seems out of harmony with any preparation for a novelist's career. Indeed, it includes a myriad of job titles along with some successes but a number of real failures too. Yet the sum total of my odd personal history has everything to do with my ending up a writer.

Even English teacher extraordinaire, Mrs. Greening's warning as she handed me my final Simi Valley High School report card on graduation day in June of 1971 with, "Trust me Mr. Pratt, you'll never make it in college with your writing skills,"* had something to do with propelling me toward this unlikely career.

Back story… As it relates to this present tale, I had the intuitive sense, a gut-feeling really, that this missing thinker of elegant letters and the written arts – the Victorian writer in question – had a similar back story experience in his life. Something of disappointment in a variety of life pursuits finally caused him to fulfill a dream of attempting to make a difference in the world as a storyteller.

If I could find this writer and his personal history, I would understand how to not only pick up where he left off, but also get inside his brain and finish the story he started ten decades ago.

I now had this cyberspace download copy of "Bard of the Themes" file before me, renamed it "Hampton of Devon" for its hero, and began to read once again a storyline my eyes first enjoyed twelve months before. It wasn't difficult to lose myself in this narrative written by a century-old beginner-novelist with no name. His work boasted of a fast pace, was expressive, and tasteful. All the things I hope to achieve as I develop a storyline.

Finishing the dozen page cursive written document, apparently scanned by some researcher for his or her own purpose, I went to the Internet search engine, "Google," thinking I could easily find the document and its source once again.

The short version is, I didn't have any luck. After hours of searching and unable to locate and trace the original Internet source, I called a local computer tech-hacker who is known simply by his first name – Bob. Bob works, no questions asked, for food and cash.

I set Bob on the trail of the IP address and domain name which I had from the original download of this one hundred year-old document. After some hours, and going on the second pizza, Bob simply said, "Sorry Jim, doesn't exist."

"It has to exist. I mean here is the stuff." I held the printed out copy in my hand. "I got the information from the Internet, right? Right here. This much printed out: http://power-think/…"

Bob shrugged his shoulders and finished off all but one slice of the pizza I had purchased for him. "Nothing there," he replied with a mouthful quickly washed down with a Diet Coke. "Look, if it existed once, it's traceable to the original source. Right?"

He wiped remains of pizza from his face, shrugged and simply said, "Can't make magic happen out of thin air, Jimmy. Sorry. It doesn't and apparently has never existed."

"Okay so I'm crazy. I'm nuts!" I was a bit upset by this point.

He just turned and sent me a facial expression which read: *You just finding that out?*

I took the remaining slice of pizza and left. I remained determined. If my mystery writer friend, who located his tale in the southwest coast of England, had finished his story, and it had become published over sixty years ago, it now resided in the realm of what is called "public domain" – meaning I could use it. But that didn't matter until I was sure that what seemed clearly "erased" from cyberspace didn't exist in print somewhere else. I needed a "hardcopy." I needed to follow copyright rules. I needed evidence that I was not losing my mind.

Once satisfied that I had in my hands a real literary treasure, lost from the world and mine alone to polish, I could develop the story out, then present it to Maryann who would in turn pitch it to the agent in New York. I had a *feeling* about this story, and in the past that meant a publishing deal.

In addition to that, the flavor of this lost writer's language and his storytelling abilities moved me. I felt both literally moved along in fascination but I was also, figuratively speaking, becoming affected by this articulate master of a moral tale. In short, I seemed to be connected to a deceased and obscure writer of great talent.

I now determined that I would need to travel to Great Britain. Perhaps on the dusty shelf of a small town library his original documents might be hiding, which of course, would make the story all the more exciting and worth telling.

As it now stood, cyberspace had given, and cyberspace had taken away. Coming to a *dead end* meant the sleuth in me was going to have to "gum shoe" it – become a literature investigator the old fashioned way; by following the paper trail, not the web page paths.

I had learned from years of writing when one follows instinct, that nagging feeling guiding you away from mere cerebral generated logic, success follows in greater degrees than all the intellectualizing one might do over a piece of work.

I wanted the completed story. And I wanted to know who this philosophical entertainer from time past was. My creative instinct whispered, "Finish the story."

I obeyed.

4
The Chamber

Lexington, Virginia

Before actually boarding the plane for Great Britain I gave a presentation to a new audience for me – a local Chamber of Commerce. Steve Densely, President of the Chamber, had noticed from a book-signing appearance I made at a local independent bookseller – The Bookery – that I was the newest of nationally published writers to call the area in, or near Lexington, Virginia, "home."

He had invited me to join the Chamber but also asked me to speak. Having heard me touch on the idea of following "instincts" for moving writing along, he asked if I would deliver the topic for the next month Chamber of Commerce breakfast titled, *"Following Instinct for Business Success."* It just so happened to be the morning of my afternoon flight to England. Something led me to believe I would benefit from this as much as audience members, so I accepted.

The day came and after a pleasant Chamber-sponsored breakfast in a restaurant, just down the street from the historic "Stonewall" Jackson home, Mr. Densley stood at the lectern and offered a flattering introduction. Taking my cue from him I stood, took my place at the podium, and began:

"I suppose this is a fitting topic for another reason. My wife and I recently moved here based on what I call the 'second voice,' but most commonly referred to as 'instinct.'

"A nagging force to investigate 'why' I felt this way produced several trips to this valley. Once I became convinced that my instincts should be obeyed, we moved. Here I am today before you talking upon the very subject I seem to use to move my strange writing lifestyle forward.*

"It seems to me that each of us is given the gift of the *second voice* at birth. Some choose to develop it more than others. An athlete at the top of his game knows what following instinct means. A business person takes risks because of it. A scientist follows intuition and makes a new discovery. A medical researcher does the same and finds a healing treatment. Police detectives follow 'hunches' to solve a case. A combat soldier learns to listen to an inner-warning and hair seems to stand up on his neck; he saves his life and those of his comrades.

"'Without further ado,' I will share with you today a story that will lead me to take a flight this afternoon from Dulles International Airport on the first leg of a trip that is all about following these *knowing feelings*. I hope this recitation may illustrate a seldom acknowledged, but slight-edge principle for those seeking success in their daily business enterprises.

"Before proceeding, I will hold up a copy of a beautifully penned cursive notation which leads me to England in search of its mysterious and unknown author. Crafted about a century ago, it seems to call out for me to find its source."

I then held a copy up for all to see. "I don't need to go to England," I half-jokingly stated, "if someone in this room can identify and connect the penmanship of this document with a name."

Polite chuckles followed.

I looked down to the front row, just feet from the podium where I stood, and noticed the intense interest with which a young lady, possibly of part Indian or Pakistani ancestry, focused upon the page. I smiled. She placed all her interest on the writing and then realizing I had noticed her, shyly turned her head away.

"This notation precedes the unknown author's actual story in very aged courier typewriter font. I will read it first and then the actual fiction he penned. The writer in question clearly was in search of creating a three act play, as the document states, but in frustration ended writing two chapters in novel form.

"Again, I have a reason to share this tale started by another, which I shall explore with you after reading it."

I began to read the original journal notes in the cursive hand of the unknown author, which I simply titled, "*The Writer.*"

5
THE WRITER

Notes: This is my sixth start to the drama, Hampton of Devon, set in this my hometown. I have taken a liberty from some history found among the writings of a family friend, now buried in the Holy Trinity Cemetery. I am finding the formatting for the Three Act Play structure a bit daunting. I had supposed it should be an easier thing to achieve. As such, my respect for true writers of action meant for the stage has reached a new height. The Bard of the Themes truly received talent from God. Perhaps I will yet realize a heavenly endowment sufficient to stand in his mighty shadow.

In Three Acts there exists what is called the "premise" which sets up ACT I. A complication or crisis follows in ACT II. Here our hero is nearly stopped in his quest. A resolution or redemption concludes the play in ACT III. Our hero wins what his heart desires.

I have plotted this thing over and over again. I have finally surrendered to put my action forth in a short fictional novel, and then hire a true playwright to convert the same to its proper structure for script and stage action. I can only hope this exercise in dramatic storytelling shall result in what I have prayed for – a fitting tribute to my ancestors, friends, and god-child and her love lost at sea. My wish for this writing is to mirror my philosophy in an entertaining way, thus garnering a wider audience for the truths affecting thought, action, and circumstance, but above all paying tribute to the noble characteristic of genuine love, without which, all victories are but hollow shells of "what might have been."

I take my cue in this attempt to influence moral thought without offending the audience from the greatest playwright of all, the Bard of the Themes. As typed by my assistant, on her new 1910 Olympic typewriter, this attempt begins thus:

HAMPTON OF DEVON

Opening Scene: It is evening and we see the silhouettes of two young lovers dashing toward the privacy they seek on a hillside overlooking the ocean in southwest Devonshire, England.

***

Summer Estate of Lord Cavandish, Southwest Coast, England 1781

They were out of breath now, having climbed the hill behind and beyond the lights of the main house. He held his hand out to her, helping her reach the crest and enjoy with him, the harbor lights below.

"My dear Miriam," he tenderly posed. "Remember when we were children living the summer months at the estate?"

"Yes," she answered sweetly. "My heart raced at the thought of coming here when school let out. I could never sleep the night before."

Just the sound of her voice had always moved something deep inside of him. This trip, across the sea to Nova Scotia and then escorting supply ships down through the American colonies could keep him away from home for two full years.

At the very least, he thought.

His ship had put up here for repairs, and it seemed that fortune had smiled upon him. He was so near to her, yet by the cruel hand of fate also so very far away. He cleared his throat and sought for the composure he required for the few words he would speak to her this night.

"There is danger in our meeting like this," he whispered.

"Isn't it delightful?" she answered gleefully.

"You are as charming as I last remember," he allowed as he cupped both her hands in his.

"And you are more handsome, and dashing too, in your Royal Navy uniform. My, Hampton! How I thought I should never see you. I had thought you would be gone to the American wars by now."

"Fortune and the grace of God smile upon us, Miriam." He thought this might be the moment his lips would meet hers but she suddenly drew away.

"So very delightful. So fortuitous," she reiterated as she spied his ship in repair docks below. "How long will the HMS South Hampton be berthed here in the harbor?"

"One week more. Two at best."

"Oh."

"Miriam, I..." he stumbled.

"Go on, Hampton. Father will soon find me gone from the party. Then he will look about to see the newest military officer in attendance also gone."

"Very well." He cleared his throat. He gazed into waiting emerald eyes that showed joy in meeting his. He took her hand and said, "Come."

They scampered to a grassy knoll just back of the store house and to their right of where they had been. An unimpeded view of the coastline north and south was offered by this slightly higher elevation.

They had separated from the nuptial celebration through stealth and ruse to find themselves beyond the gaze of the party goers, servants, and others. Past the vegetable garden, through a gate where an ancient stone wall shielded them from any view of the festivities going on at the estate of Lord Cavandish, Duke of Devon, they knew their time away would soon be noticed. This, the official family gathering to honor her elder brother's betrothal to the Lady of Newcastle, put Miriam next in line for arranged marriage.

And he, the son of groundskeeper Albert Allen Rhodes, was not the man Lord Cavandish had in mind. This heaviness weighed upon his mind and caused him to further search for the words which would invite her to disobey family protocols and time honored tradition.

"In my mind," he began.

"I love this time of year," she squealed, pretending not to hear him speak. She twirled about, allowing Hampton to view her splendid figure, teasing him though adorned in modest but womanly fashions from London. "Last time we were here we were much younger, and you kissed me. Remember?"

Is she playing with my mind? he wondered as eyes locked. He smiled, nodded and drew closer to her.

"Wouldn't it be grand if..." She suddenly stopped and looked at her fine young love so resplendent in dress uniform. *How can I tell him what I must do when my heart tells me to do anything he asks me to?*

"If?" he asked as he cupped her chin in his hand and gazed once again into eyes. "If?"

"Oh look!" she declared with a pointed hand to the sky. "Look at the meteors streaking across the sky!" she said happily as she plopped to the ground with an invitation for Hampton to follow her. "A touch of cold air for such a splendid summer eve, don't you agree, Hampton?"

He slid to her side and gently offered his arm around delicate shoulders. Just the touch of her exposed arm thrilled him, but he must pretend to be interested in this heavenly light show now.

"Didn't you just love it when we stole away and watched the northern lights, and the stars at night, and the only sounds were our hearts, along with the chirpings of crickets and such," she said. "It was so much easier being a child. I wish I were a child again," she sighed, snuggling up to him.

"Aye I loved it. I loved it very much."

"And now, years later, here we are again. Hampton..."

"Yes, Miriam. What is it?"

She shook her head and he thought he detected moisture fill her eyes. "I look into the night sky, and know there must be a creator of it all who is good, and kind, and has a plan for me; for us... I want..."

Once again she was caught in despair for desperately wishing she could say what she felt. She wanted to stay here with him, and not be in *there*. *There*, where a foreshadowing of marriage awaited, along with the Duke of Cornwall's son and at least two other "back up" suitors of the upper class she knew her father had arranged.

"I believe, Miriam," Hampton simply replied.

"You do?" she asked. "You believe there is a plan for us?"

"I do. I know a creator gave us this," he answered waving his free arm across the sky. "To give us hope," he added. "He showed us that we are partakers of all He has. He simply paints the sky with his power and asks of us each, 'What part of this shall I give to you, my child?'"

She shivered and nodded as if in agreement and her gaze turned to his with solemnity and resolve. "I will ask for my part then."

"I too, shall ask for my part. Miriam, I have always loved..."

"Miriam!" a deeply disturbed voice rang from the shadows. "Miriam! In God's name where have you gone! Miriam! You had better report at once! Father's patience is waning."

ENSIGN HAMPTON'S QUARTERS

Scene 2: We see Hampton in his cot. He is tossing and turning as he awakens to a new day. He tries to ignore a knock upon his door.

***

Hampton roused from the dream that replayed their short visit of the night before. He woke slowly to the dawn and the realization that he had come so very close to asking her to wait for his return from war. He had intended to declare his full and undying love for Miriam, the daughter of the Duke of Devon, and his cherished soul-mate from childhood.

"But I am a groundskeeper's son," he muttered, at the sound of a knock upon the door of his bedchamber.

"Sir. Breakfast is served," came the high pitched voice of his teenage seaman steward and aide, Johnnie Camp.

"If there is a God, a great Creator, and if He knows my thoughts, then I swear I will have the hand of Miriam Cavandish in marriage. And I shall declare my intentions before the day is through," he determined under his breath.

"A notice, marked 'urgent' just arrived for you, sir. Shall I hold on to it or slide it under the door?"

"Slip it through, if you will, Johnnie."

One of the newest junior officers in the British navy was tormented by the thoughts of leaving her again. He had grown up on the on the summer estate of Lord Cavandish, and his heart had belonged to the fair Miriam from the first time he had laid eyes upon her. That was twenty years ago.

His naval officer training had lasted nearly two years and now that fortune had his warship, the HMS South Hampton, docked here for repairs, this summer home for the House of Cavandish also meant he could, with stealth, see his beloved; or ruin his naval career.

There was irony in being named for the seventeenth century Earl of Southampton and serving on the ship named for him. His given name of Hampton Allen Rhodes, was meant to honor the same Earl who had directly saved his great-grandfather's life in the Virginia colony also named for the famed Lord Southampton in the 1600's.

Hampton was in love with the daughter of Catherine Southampton, wife of Lord Cavandish. Both had links to the same family tree as the famous colonizer. So Miriam's links to this history were through blood, his links to her family line and history were established through heroics and service. Lord Cavandish, Duke of Devon was the same man who had recommended him to the Naval Academy. This blend of ironies was not lost on him

It is in God's hand now. I should be grateful, but he thought he had gotten rid of me, he added as he handled the envelope addressed to him.

If he, Ensign Rhodes, was to believe in fate and the alignment of stars, he could clearly see the hand of divine fortune crafting a marriage to his beloved Miriam Southampton Cavandish of Devon.

Last night, as she fled into the darkness, she had finally revealed her heart to him with the words, *"Yes. The answer is yes, Hampton!"*

"I will have her!" he spoke aloud as he paced the floor in thought. He turned the envelope over and slipped a finger under the flap. He noticed the seal of wax was stamped with that of the House of Cavandish.

"Well then. Here it is," he sighed. Though Lord Cavandish, Duke of Devon, had offered to open doors to the groundskeeper's son so that he, Hampton, might join the honored military class of England, he knew full well that the door opened for him did not include marriage to a Duke's daughter.

His position as an Ensign in the Royal Navy did not promise her the station in life, nor the comforts, of her Lady upbringing, as her father the Duke, required.

Noticing the date was that of this day, he read:

Ensign Rhodes,

You are a fine young fellow. However, I cannot allow your pursuit of affection for my only daughter to continue. Either you cut this affair off now, or I shall be forced to use my influence with Vice Admiral Wood. I'm very sure you shall grow during a six or seven year post to the East Indies, or at war among the American dissidents to the Crown.
Choose well your path lad, and you shall yet arrive to the destiny

*designed by God and for which he has preserved your life thus far. Re-
mind yourself of your station in life and aspire to nothing more. Yield
to reason of the mind, Ensign Rhodes, and do not indulge this passion of
the heart for my daughter. As you do you shall always find yourself in
good graces of those who may control your future advancement in His
Majesty's service.*

*I have a fondness for you and your father's household. But do not
misinterpret that fondness to mean acceptance into a position or state
of affairs in society to which you do not belong.*

*In His Majesty's Service,
Lord Cavandish, Duke of Devon*

The unwritten, but implied threat, to use his influence to have him
permanently stationed far from England, and for as long as it took to
break up the love affair he shared with Miriam was, after all, real and
doable.

He angrily tossed the letter aside, went to the mirror and applied
water from the wash bowl along with lathered soap to his face.

"He must have risen early to insist upon this special delivery,"
Hampton said aloud as he studied the stubble he would clear with a sharp
edged blade. He stopped as he studied the man's face mirrored back to
him. *Why don't I just finish it?* he thought as he applied the shaving
razor to his neck.

Ensign Rhodes knew he must choose now; resign his commission and
seek a way into the good graces of the Duke, or risk losing Miriam for
life.

His other love and dream had always been the sea. The tales his father had told him of his forbearers and their daring in the British sea
services during which the great colonies in America had first been established, had always caused him to want to be there; far beyond the
confines and dullness of life as a groundkeeper's son in Devonshire.

Which love should I choose?

These thoughts tormented him, as did his breaking heart, and yet if
he followed his heart he would give up the long cherished dreams from
boyhood to serve nobly at sea. If he chose the thoughts and dreams of
Navy service he would lose real meaning in life; his love for a fine
woman.

He took the razor and began to apply it against his skin. Stroke of
the blade, cleanse with water in the bowl. Stroke again, cleanse again.
He can't keep our love from being what it is! he demanded silently as he
finished the job.

Wiping his face dry with a hand towel, Hampton dressed, straightened
his collar, and stood to look at the British officer reflected back to
him from the mirror. He recalled her final words to him: *"Yes. The answer is yes, Hampton!"*

As it now seemed, he had but one choice open to him...

6
CHAMBER MADE

"And here is where the mystery document comes to an end," I said.

I had looked up occasionally to see if the Chamber members were dozing, walking out, fidgeting. I was surprised to find myself at the end of the reading of *Hampton of Devon* with silence. Even table servers joined in, standing around the back of the room waiting to find out how Hampton would pull off the impossible task of keeping his Navy career from being destroyed by an angry father, and achieving marriage to Miriam, the love of his life.

"That's it?" an attractive businesswoman asked. "You aren't going to tell us how it ends?" she asked in charming southern drawl.

I smiled, shook my head and shuffled my papers as I prepared to end my speech. In finishing I explained, "You have been an amazing audience. It is validating to feel the respectful attention which you paid to *Hampton of Devon*. But the reading was not the point of the presentation," I added.

"The *point* resides in a fact that an unknown writer followed his instinct long ago, and then disappearing, he left ACT I of a warm-hearted story of love and conflict to be finished later. This is all I have to go on, and now my instinct tells me there is something here to finish, something I did not even intentionally look for."

I again noticed the particularly attentive young lady in the front row; in fact sitting just a few feet from the podium she seemed to hang on my every word. I smiled, and continued.

"I found the mystery writer's *Hampton of Devon* one day on the Internet, saved it in a computer file and it came forth just months ago in a synchronistic way which will now take me to England in search of the original writer's identity.

"Let me propose a series of rhetorical questions. Given a strong internal intuition to travel to England in pursuit of this story, should I risk losing time and money on the speculative venture? What if an agent doesn't like it? What if I am delusional with regards to the value I believe exists in this partial novel meant one hundred years ago for a stage play? I have no buyer. What should I do?"

"I'll buy a copy!" a cute mid-aged Hispanic waitress yelled from the back.

"Me too," called a table server standing next to her.

The audience chuckled but seemed to be enjoying this spontaneous survey I had undertaken.

"I've got to know, Mr. Pratt," whispered a matronly but smartly dressed businesswoman from the front row, "does Hampton get the girl?"

"How do I know unless I follow instincts?"

Laughter.

"See, we are all given opportunities to write our own scripts in life, and daily – at least daily – each of us will get a small whisper we call gut instinct, intuition, that nagging sense tugging at us to leave our comfort zone and go expand the thought, whether in business, personal affairs, or matters of the heart.

"Where business instinct is concerned, I'm convinced many may get the same nudging regarding a matter. Inventions happen and you recall having had the same idea. Someone acted upon it and won the patent and business interests. You say to yourself, 'That was my idea. If only I had…'

"A story-line is given to several at once, and a few act upon it. New novels, movies, and non-fiction then result in what seems to the readers and viewers a plethora of writers some- how conspiring together to deliver topics so connected, and apparently all in a matter of months of each other.*

"How does this occur? I haven't the time now to go in to detail, but the 'second voice' is the slight edge which determines projects coming forward in the precise time in which other factors appear to propel them into the realm we call success. 'What might have been,' is not the statement that should define our lives, but too often is the case.

"May I be so bold to inquire by show of hands, how many would like to know how the story I have just read, ends?"

Every hand went up along with spontaneous chatter and laughter.

"This now shall serve as my official test marketing and survey. I will go then, to England, risk my entire life savings and reputation on your word."

Chamber President Steve Densley arose, put his arm around me and said, "You aren't sticking me with that guilt trip, Mr. Pratt. We are appreciative for the vivid presentation." He presented me with a copy of the history of Lexington and its Chamber of Commerce.

"Thank you. I promise to report back with what famed radio personality Paul Harvey would call, '…the rest of the story.' Then if you judge it a winner, I'll take that to the bank and you'll be off the hook." I waved to the crowd and left the Chamber to its business.

I could not have known it then, but this Chamber-made event would impact the story I shared with them in a way I could have never imagined, and for which I would travel thou- sands of miles in the next two days.

7
SCENE CHANGE

I had a quick delivery to make of autographed books requested by an advisor to the incoming Freshman Class at the famed Virginia Military Institute just blocks away. I chose to walk rather than backtrack to my car.

It would be a fifteen minute walk up the hill from Main Street, on to East Washington, then up to Lee Avenue. Strolling past the entrance to adjacent Washington & Lee University, and then up the long circular drive to the entry of the fortress-like military college, was another five to ten minutes.

I was delighted to be invited to speak at the beginning of the term for the Freshman Class at VMI, though the actual speaking event wasn't scheduled until next month, after my return from England.

The instructor in charge of this event invited me after hearing my reading for a Washington & Lee Layburn Library event on the World War Two battle for the Philippines, as depicted in *Ticket Home*, still a popular novel six years after first being published.

I had determined that my coming presentation of military history would take the approach of a "Three Act Play," with the Parker brothers of *Ticket Home* developing the drama, to show how we all have "Three Acts" scripted for our lives, whether by default or through deliberate planning.

I was half way down the block from the restaurant and ready to turn the corner to Washington Street, when I detected a gentle female voice call out my name.

"Mr. Pratt? Hello – Mr. Pratt?"

I turned to see a familiar face from the front row of the event just concluded, nervously seeking to catch my attention. She seemed shy, unsure of herself. I waved for her to join me.

"Yes? How may I help you?" I asked with a smile as she drew close.

"I, uh... I'm rather interested in the story you read moments ago, Mr. Pratt," she timidly answered.

"You have a British accent."

"Yes sir, Mr. Pratt."

"Are you going my way?"

"Toward the University?"

I nodded.

"Yes. I am headed to the chapel. But if this is an inconvenience, I could..."

"Nonsense! No inconvenience at all. I'm walking right past on my way to VMI. We can walk together and talk about the story if you like."

"Oh... Yes! Marvelous!" She suddenly became self-conscious about her excitement and came back down to a charming level of apprehensiveness. "Are you sure it wouldn't be too much trouble?" she humbly asked again.

I tipped my head in the direction and waited for her to join in step with me as we started north to the campus area. "I don't know your name."

"Oh yes. I am happy to say I have the name of the young lady in your story."

"Miriam Cavandish?" I replied with surprise.

"Rhodes is my mother's maiden appellation, and my father's…" She smiled, but didn't finish.

"Astonishing!" I breathed.

"Yes. Quite," she quietly voiced.

"Hum. Well Miriam, I think this is quite an interesting coincidence, wouldn't you say?"

"I absolutely adored the story and somehow, it sounded so familiar I just had to ask you how and where you came upon it; if you don't mind."

"Not at all. Tell me a bit about yourself. Are you enrolled in a three or four year degree program?" I asked.

She smiled. "On a special assignment, actually. Connected to the Lee Chapel."

I didn't pursue "what kind" of assignment she referred to but asked, "Why Washington & Lee?"

"Oh, it is so American. Founded by your first President, George Washington and overseen later by the great American Civil War General, Robert E. Lee. Then it is in Virginia and I am tracing some of my English ancestors who immigrated after your American Revolution. My work takes me between the chapel and the library. I was happy to get my wish to come here."

"It does carry the traditions of what being American means. I agree it is a charming school with a lot to offer."

I was intrigued at not only her background, but her name and the fact that I was headed to England that very evening. "You must be surprised as I am to find two of the names I used in the reading this morning combined with your own," I added.

"Yes quite. I felt so very connected as you read. Perhaps it is my British/Indian heritage and love of reading."

I nodded. Though curious, I would ask her about her Indian heritage and surname later. "Then shall I share again how I came upon the story?"

"Oh would you?"

"Very well," I answered. "Here goes." We walked. I talked, rehearsing the entire matter regarding my strange discovery and the dead end I had arrived at.

She was as sweet and entirely as innocent a person as one could find. It was refreshing and I felt sure I was with someone as pure and genuine as the Miriam from the story; a rare personal commodity found in any age and time. She could not be more than in her late teens or early twenties, but the way she carried herself made her seem twice that age.

We were approaching the university chapel and the entrance to the campus itself. I would be parting with Miriam to continue on a few hundred yards more to the east and up the hill to the fortress-like Virginia Military Institute.

"Now tell me again. You come from a mixed heritage; Indian mother and an English father?" I ventured, knowing it was the other way around.

"Rhodes, my mother's name is how I am known on family records. My father's name is not used at his request since the tide of bigotry has not yet calmed in our small English village. He is a mighty man of faith, in the traditions of our Indian fore bearers," she said, voice trailing off.

I was delighted that this sweet girl felt more comfortable and had so easily become trusting as a friend would. Her pained expression regarding bigotry touched me.

She continued, "There is more to it than that, but I'm afraid my pure Sikh grandparent's were none too happy either about a marriage where my mother of English heritage married their son. And where else, but in Devon, England. But then when it is a matter of the heart what can well-intentioned and reasoning parents do?"

"Well said, Miriam! And from Devon too?" I added rhetorically. I was now speechless at her recounting family history with its Romeo and Juliet similarity to *Hampton of Devon's* opening narrative. The coincidence of this young woman's background was probably no more than that, but it made my day to feel something confirm to me that my instinct was on track, and that today's trip was the right thing to do.

"I would like to know the ending of the story, if you find one, Mr. Pratt."

"Miriam, I promise. You shall be the first to know of the results of my research."

"If it isn't too much trouble, Mr. Pratt, may I have a copy of your text, *Hampton of Devon*? I would keep it safe. It made me feel so at home."

We had come to the campus chapel built after the Civil War by then President of the University, Robert E. Lee. I hesitated. I rarely share unfinished work, but then this had come from the Internet in the first place.

"Certainly. Why don't you go to my official website, click 'Email the Author' and put your name in the subject line. I'll send a copy as an attachment." I then jotted down my website address and was ready to part company.

"Miriam," I found myself saying. "I have an impression to leave this with you." I pulled the print-out from my satchel. "'Hampton of Devon' for the beautiful Miriam of Devonshire," I added with a slight waist-line bow along with a gentlemanly nod of the head. She received it like a child at Christmas as I handed her the *Hampton of Devon* print out.

"Mr. Pratt. I promise to cherish this and take good care of it. This isn't your only copy, is it?" she excitedly asked.

"It is. But I have it also in a file on my laptop computer. No worries," I replied. "You take good care of it. If my computer crashes and I lose the file, I know where to find you, right?"

"Oh yes, Mr. Pratt! Thank you, Mr. Pratt! I can't wait to read it!" she exclaimed.

"Perhaps we can visit a month from now when I return from the 'mother country.'"

She giggled. "I'd love that. Good hunting to you, Mr. Pratt," she added.

"Thank you, Miriam. I must be off." I bowed once again, with an added dramatic flare.

She curtsied, which caused me a serious amount of pleasure. Her child-like "curtsy" was so very proper, dignified, and serious, as if it were her everyday lady manners and upbringing in an English age, long ago dead to the modern world.

I heard her call out as I walked away, "Thank you again, Mr. Pratt."

The absence of guile in this young person left me happy for meeting her. "We'll be seeing you, Miriam," I replied as I turned. She was no where in sight. I then saw the door to the chapel closing and smiled. *A good person*, I thought.

I now drew near to the famed citadel-like VMI Administration building. I entered the front lobby, was met by my host, and soon finished the business requiring my attention.

I was eager to get on the road and headed to my first leg of the journey, a flight from Dulles International, just outside Washington DC, for JFK in New York City.

I could feel myself drawn across the Atlantic and hoped to soon know the name of my benefactor; the unknown writer who I had connected so thoroughly with. "Hampton and Miriam..." I said to myself. "You just keep on talking."

8

"Go To Dee Center"

I awoke from my scene-by-scene dreamland revisit of the past two days, including the nightmare parts of a journey my wife wouldn't believe, and one which I wasn't sure I should journal.

I got up from my well deserved snooze, went to the window, and peered through the curtain to see a cold and fog shrouded street below. "Jack the Ripper," I voiced, recalling the history of this neighborhood near Gloucester Road. With that thought, I decided my hunger pangs would best be served ordering from room service.

After placing the order for authentic English fish and chips, not the Skipper's fast food variety I am used to, I sat on the edge of the bed plotting my next series of moves.

Give Mark Kastleman a call, suddenly came to mind. I looked at the digital clock on the nightstand. *Six hours difference. He'll be in the office by now.* As pals we sometimes collaborate on speaking and writing projects in the self-improvement world, but almost always enjoy as many chats about the latest in life as often as there are spare moments in a week to share them.

This was a good excuse to try this international cell phone I purchased specifically for my travel here in Great Britain. Having some time on my hand before room service arrived, I gave Mark a call. In seconds I heard his comforting voice.

"Is this Mark Kastleman, Esquire?" I said with an attempt at feigned English eloquence.

"Jimmy! What a surprise! I thought you fell off the edge of the world!"

"Mark, good to hear a friendly voice," I replied sleepily. "Just arrived this morning. Staying at the Montana Hotel. I wanted you to have the cell phone number I'll be using while here."

"You sound beat. You in Montana?"

"No. London."

"Oh yeah! The trip to England. So how'd it go so far?"

"'Curiouser and curiouser,'" I replied.

"What?" he laughed.

I pondered my reply. Did Mark need to hear this? It still seemed rather unbelievable to me. "Alice in Wonderland," I finally returned.

"Jim? You okay?" he chuckled.

"The rabbit in the fairy tale Alice chased... the one holding the pocket watch shouting, *'I'm late, I'm late for a very important date?'* The major differences between me and the rabbit is, I would have chased Alice and I carry a Blackberry, not a pocket watch," I said with a yawn. "I'd still be late though."

He obviously didn't have a clue where this was headed, but if I played the comedic pause line well, I could always elicit some laughter from my sober-minded friend.

"Soooo... I take it you've had an interesting trip?" Mark questioned. "Happy accidents?" he asked light-heartedly.

"Hummm... Then some. Might be something in them for you."

"All ears," he answered.

I explained that I was growing concerned that if the kind of events which happened during my travel to England happened over here, I might not make it back home to Virginia. "Three incidents challenging my travel across the pond," I finished.

"Meaning?" he asked.

"In *Wonderland*... Alice woke up and it was a dream. This is real."

His great listening ear was just what I needed right now, especially with regards to one singular phrase uttered at JFK yesterday that kept playing over and over again in my mind.

I began by relating my success with the Lexington Chamber of Commerce and the sharing of the *Hampton of Devon* story, and then meeting an enchanting young woman from England with the heroin's name in the story.

"So many coincidences, as if it was meant for me to come here; now... Today. Yet peppered with incredible complications; like warnings or something."

"ACT II stuff," Mark chuckled.

"I hope so. That means 'resolution' for the hero is just on the horizon. If I can just score quickly by finding who the mystery author of the Hampton story is, I would feel more at ease."

I then launched in to a travel expose' with a desire to ask Mark what he felt about the encounter with a strange but helpful man at JFK, who seemed to appear out of nowhere when I needed him most.

"From the time I entered I-84 north in the Shenandoah Valley headed to Dulles International in Sterling, to the connecting flight at JFK in New York, I experienced more craziness than should be legal," I told Mark.

∾∾

My trip up the heart of Virginia's Shenandoah Valley from just outside Lexington had left a gash in the hood of my car. That stressed me out a bit, since bullets from handguns don't generally strike the center of a driver's windshield after ricocheting from a hood ornament. There was no explanation for that, except the squashed lead evidence I turned over to the State Trooper just outside of Front Royal after he pulled me over for the shattered windshield.

I showed him what I had dug out of the collapsed windshield with my pocket-knife. He admitted that it was rare, but noted that shooting ranges out in the farm land sometimes offered stray bullets.*

"What goes up, always comes down," he said as he placed the evidence in a plastic bag. "I'll call for a tow truck," he added.

"A tow truck?"

"Unless you want to place the call. Do you have Triple 'A' roadside coverage?"

I nervously dug through my wallet. "Whew. Got it," I said.

"Follow me to the turn out," he replied.

I did as the trooper instructed and to make a long story short, called the automobile club, got a mobile auto glass service to come out, and by the time I was back on the road, I had ninety minutes to get to Dulles for the recommended early check-in.

I got to Long Term Parking with thirty minutes to spare before my flight. *Glad I'm only carrying my laptop bag on board,* I allowed in self-talk. I hustled to the terminal with bags in tow.

Checking in my large bag at the curbside with the Sky Cap, I paid the obligatory tip, and got my seating confirmation. Running up the moving escalator stairs to security screening, I was glad to find the line was short.

I sent my laptop through the x-ray scanners as a TSA officer signaled for me to walk through the sniffing machines designed to weed out terrorists. Explosive devices and people handling them usually carry a residue upon their cloths or skin. I was immediately weeded out by a "puff" of air blown on me as I passed through the machine for added screening which included a "pat-down" leaving me with little personal dignity or time for the flight.

I wondered how this could happen as I watched my laptop being examined. "Careful with that," I shouted to the TSA bag screener.

I wish I had remained a bit more reserved as a Dulles Airport Authority Police Sergeant approached me and demanded I put my hands behind my back. I complied. Another pat-down accompanied. My pocket-knife appeared and I was suddenly in a world of trouble.

"This is for your own safety, sir. I will need you to remain silent unless we begin questioning you," he said as he snapped handcuffs on my wrists.

"I'm not a terrorist. Do I look like a terrorist?" I shot back.

"No one said anything about terrorists, sir. You have something on your mind?" the sergeant replied.

"Yes, I do. I am a wreck. I'm stressed. I dodged a bullet not ninety minutes ago, and now this. I will miss a flight. I want out of here."

"Dodged a bullet?" the sergeant asked. "Explain."

I quickly re-lived the handling of a bullet that fell unexpectedly from the sky, lodging itself in my car's windshield, and thus the reason why the pocket-knife was still in my pocket.

I gazed around at the three officers who surrounded me now. All carried the facial expressions: "Yeah, *right.*" The sergeant asked me if I wouldn't like to take a ride with him to my car and show him the damage.

"I'll miss my flight," I answered.

"Yes you will," he replied.

He asked a fellow officer, who was handling a hungry looking mastiff, to accompany us.

"Are the cuffs necessary? I mean, this is rather embarrassing."

"You famous or something?"

"Or something," I answered.

"Then the cuffs stay on."

The walk to the curbside from the screening gate, along with people turning their heads to stare, was the longest part of the heart-pounding ordeal.

"Look Mommy. The policeman caught a bad man!" a little boy shouted above the din of announcements and general airport noise.

"I'm a good-guy, kid."

His mother didn't seem impressed by my answer and the police officer just nudged me forward. The thought crossed my mind to say something dramatic like: "I'll have your job," but I'd been a cop and didn't want his job.*

Upon arriving at the curbside I was instructed to sit in the back of the patrol car which pulled up to greet me. A short ride later I was freed from my cuffs and asked to unlock my car.

"Can't. My keys are in the laptop bag back at the screening counter," I answered.

The sergeant rolled his eyes, sure he was dealing with a very stupid criminal, radioed, and soon another officer appeared with my bag. I opened a zipper pouch, and pulled my keys from the bag. "Here you go," I said as I extended the keys.

The dog handler seemed to enjoy the tour of the car interior. The German Shepherd was so excited at what he found as he sniffed and barked at the windshield area of the dashboard, that he urinated on the driver seat upholstery.

"They do that sometimes," the canine unit officer chuckled. "Looks like just the windshield, Sergeant. Could have been a slug from a 9mm the *purp* reported," he cynically added.

"I'm not a purp."

"Well, shall I let my German Shepard back in the car?" the canine officer sarcastically asked. "Maybe he can do a second number while he checks things out a bit more thoroughly," he finished to the approving grins from his fellow officers.

These guys must be awfully bored, I thought.

A call to the Virginia Highway Patrol finally resolved the issue after one hour. "Our apologies, Mr. Pratt. It happens sometimes."

"Yeah. Thanks," I said, as I walked back into the terminal, a free man. I went to the nearest airport convenience store, purchased the strongest soap and baby wipes I could find, and went back to my car to clean up after the dog. After all, I had already missed my flight and was considering bagging this whole trip and going home. I'd seen this movie before; a bad beginning always seemed to promise more of the same.

Opportunity number one to turn back, I paused. *Naw...* I decided. This was not a bad omen, just life, and so I went ahead.

After putting in a cell phone call to my travel agent, asking her to reschedule my flights including a stay over in Manhattan, I cleaned out the car, leaving the windows partially cracked open.

Staying over a day in New York City will help me regain my composure and nix the bad karma, I considered in silent thought.

I boarded the Delta flight to JFK and after a half hour the flight attendant's voice came over the intercom with this apology: "Captain Nemo and crew thank you for your patience. There seems to be a small problem with the wing's flap controls. Maintenance has assured us that as soon as all are checked we will be cleared for departure."*

"Captain Nemo? I thought that was a submarine captain," I chuckled to the passenger seated next to me. She tried a smile in response.

After another thirty minutes, the airline pilot announced: "Hello, this is the Captain speaking. I apologize for this delay, but it seems our altimeter isn't working quite right. I promise that as soon as we have it checked we will continue our take off procedures."

"Well; wings, altitude gauge. No biggie right," I continued to my seat-mate. She responded with raised eyebrows of concern.

"Don't worry," I counseled. "As soon as he finds out this isn't a sea port, but an airport, we'll get the right captain and be out of here."

She laughed a nervous and polite laugh.

Thirty minutes later, after another announcement that we were lining up on the correct runway, the engines screamed and we were thrust back in our seatbacks and soon airborne. "Guess Captain Nemo can fly," I assured with a grin.

Laughter erupted, from not only my heretofore silent Row 6 seating companion, but from several people who had obviously been listening in to the one-sided exchange.

"Hello, this is Flight Attendant Arial," a voice came over the plane's PA system. She began to offer the customary safety speech and then said something that really caught my attention:

"Please note that the seat cushions may be used as a flotation device should that unlikely event be required. Captain Nemo asks you to remain seated with seat belts securely fastened. We will *probably* reach our flying altitude of 30,000 feet. Once we reach…"

"Probably!" I blurted for everyone to hear. "Floatation device? *Arial?*" I then quietly said to my new friend sipping from her water bottle.*

She spit out the water and laughed loudly. We both continued in this state of humor until tears came. Several more seated passengers offered chuckles. *And I thought Jeanne was the only one headed to Adventure Land,* I said in more self-talk, designed at comic relief.

Here was yet another sign that this day was, and probably would continue to be highly unusual. I would have turned back and gone home, but I was strapped in without a parachute.

Arriving in Manhattan, I checked in with my wife, gave her an update, promised to pray for her travel and asked the same for the remainder of mine. Telling her about the troubles from Lexington to Dulles in Sterling, Virginia, I received no sympathy whatsoever.

"Only you could pull that one off!" she laughed. "Captain Nemo…"

"No really! It really really happened. Cross my heart!"

"Okie dokie. My flight was just announced. I'm leaving Denver and should be in LA in two hours or so. Want me to call to see if you need bail?" She actually laughed again.

"Well, yes call. I might need it. I love you. Thanks for letting me go to England."

"I love you too. Thanks for sending me to Disneyland."

"Enjoy the Tea Cups," I said to a click. "Hello? Jeanne?"

My agent booked a room at the Ritz-Carlton, on 50 Central Park South. I reasoned that I deserved to pamper myself after the Dulles Airport stress. Taking a copy of my latest manuscript, *When the Last Leaf Falls,* I decided to enjoy the warmth of a perfect late summer evening in Manhattan. People were out, there were well-lit areas with park benches, and though the thought crossed my mind that locking myself behind a closed door in a hotel might be the wiser choice, I disobeyed.

I ambled across the street, found a quiet and off-the-beaten-path Central Park bench in a well lit area close to the west side, and began to read. There was a gully off to my right, a picnic table not far from me on my left, and a man seated there seemingly enjoying a newspaper.

Good. Got some company. Muggers like people less guarded, I reasoned. I began to read, red pen at the ready.

No sooner had I flipped through a couple of manuscript pages than the feeling of being watched came over me. I turned. Two men soon appeared at the edge of a ravine; just over my right shoulder. Inquiring glances my way with their positions in shrubs obscuring them from the man at the table, gave them away. The men talked in whispers, and I did as well; under my breath of course. "Cops."

My two decade old police officer training instincts led me to the conclusion I had inadvertently entered a drug bust or sting operation of some kind. I remained calm and wondered if getting up and leaving might help, or if by acting their willing accomplice through a devil-may-care nonchalant attitude might be the better strategy. As that thought crossed my mind, a man appeared suddenly on my left, joining the other man at the picnic table.

Before I could say, "I'm outta here," the two men from the gully charged up and past my bench with guns drawn, while five others appeared out of nowhere, all yelling "Get down! Get down! Police! Don't move! Get down!"*

I obeyed, but not until I was knocked from behind by a narcotics undercover officer, handcuffed, and told to remain silent. I wondered, as my face was plastered to the park lawn, if England wouldn't be safer.

Soon enough, the error was discovered and my innocence was again established, just as it had been at Dulles International. I was released, apologized to, and given the card of the officer who seemed genuinely worried I might press charges.

I said, "Officer Anzilotti, I was once a reserve police officer in Southern California, and though I didn't make it a career, I still feel the brotherhood."*

We enjoyed the good-natured banter about cops and the strange world they seem to live in before I bid his friends, the nice narcotics undercover officers, good-bye with, "Have a nice day."

Anzilotti stuck around, and seemed visibly relaxed knowing I would not add any "false arrest" paperwork to his file. He kindly invited me to dinner, which I politely turned down with, "I would love to accept but I have a growing aversion to being around guns and cuffs, although my wife should be calling any minute to see if I need bail money."

The phone rang. I pulled it from my pocket. I heard, "Hi honey? I'm safe in LA. Tim's here to pick me up. You staying out of trouble?"

"It's my wife," I said in a whisper as we shook hands. Officer Anzilotti laughed and waved goodbye, as I answered, "Of course not. It's what I do."

"Funny."

More, "I love yous" followed as I walked toward the Ritz, *not* telling her the truth of what had just happened.

I gathered my bags and immediately called British Airways and was able to get the last first Class Seat available on a flight leaving in two hours from JFK. This short Manhattan stay, along with the Central Park incident, was opportunity number two presenting itself to me as a *sign* to turn back and go home.

I thought, *I'm going to beat this bad ju ju and get to England.* I was now in the parking garage, in my rental car, a Chevy Malibu convertible with the top down. I needed my high blood pressure meds. I reached into my satchel, grabbed a pill and swallowed. Funny thing is, in my mental state the relaxant looked exactly like the blood pressure med I wanted to down. Already fatigued, I made my way across Manhattan to Queens and began to feel a light-headed silliness that caught me off guard.

"I need to remember to take them in the evening," I counseled myself. I focused on I-678 that led to JFK. I had an hour before my flight and needed to return the Chevy Malibu rental car. Returning a rental car at JFK with the country's worst airport signs makes it easy to cause you to drive in circles as you search for the "Rental Car Return Here" sign, especially when you are drugged.

Frustrated, and after two circular attempts without success, I finally stopped curbside at the British Airways check-in and asked a uniformed Airport Police Officer for instructions to the car rental exit.

Blown off by his shrug of the shoulder, along with *"Ya can't park here, buddy. Now move along,"* I ignored him when he got a call to head inside. I watched for a few seconds to make sure he wasn't hanging around to cite me, then got out of the convertible and nearly fell to the ground from sudden dizziness.

Hitting my head against the car door really hurt. "The BP meds never did that to me before," I muttered.

I squinted and tried to focus on a middle-aged bearded, turban topped, baggage manager from India, who suddenly, and with courtesy I had not yet experienced on this trip, appeared seemingly from nowhere to my rescue.

"How wheel I be assisting you?" he kindly offered.

He helped me back to the car. Recalling what I had wanted to ask when I had pulled up seconds before, I inquired, "I'm kind of in a hurry to get this car back so I don't miss my flight. I can't seem to find the exit for the car rental return. Can you help me?"

He smiled and then pointedly said in slow, deliberate instructive but Indian accented English, "You wheel see a sigh-een. When you see dee sigh-een, do NOT go to dee left. Do NOT go to dee right. Goooo...," he said, with a lengthy emphasis, "to dee center," he ordered with a gestured use of his right hand. "In dee center, you wheel find your vay." *

I smiled, knew I was probably in deep trouble, wished my wife were here to do the driving, got back in the car, pulled out, and began looking for "dee center."

I soon found the sign and did not go to the left, or the right, but as the road forked both ways, I stayed in the middle as the kind Sikh dressed airport baggage handler instructed. Strangely it worked, and I found myself pulling in to the Avis rental return line in seconds.

"You wheel be having a little fender bender?" the turban-topped check-in clerk voiced as he pointed to a scratch I hadn't noticed. "That wheel be costing." He walked around the car making notes.

Still woozy I answered, "I didn't have any fender-bender. Are you related to..." but then just grabbed my luggage. "Whatever," I added with a forced smile. *I am either suffering from some sort of drug induced Bombay, India rental car dream, or I died in Central Park and...*

"You wheel be going to dee Terminal?" the clerk voiced, breaking me from my reverie.

Terminal? I quickly wondered what my wife would be told about my death. I answered, "Yes. Dee Terminal."

He replied with a gesture of the hand. "You wheel be wanting to go... to dee rental center," he said pointing. "Dee shuttle wheel be taking you to dee terminal," he finished.

Soon the shuttle arrived, I picked up the luggage, tossed it aboard, and to my pleasant surprise found myself at the British Airways terminal, and easily made my way to the check-in gate. I enjoyed immediate Platinum Flyer privileges, and soon boarded ahead of the crowd, finding myself in a cozy cushioned First Class seat.

"I like the British," I decided. "I even like the people they colonized," I added in reference to the helpful Indian baggage manager and his cousin, the nice Avis rental car check-out man.

"So that's it," I finished.

Mark had been patient. "Where's that punch line you promised? The one I've been hanging on to this call for twenty minutes to hear?"

"I said it already."

"Huh?"

"Okay. Let me dramatize it. Before I knew it we were airborne and I was dozing off into a pleasant and restful muscle relaxant induced place that traveling thus far had eluded me. The last words I remember going through my sedated, though over-active mind – and I swear to this Mark – were in a stilted India-flavored English accent: *Go to dee center. In dee center you wheel find your way.*"

Silence.

"Hello? Mark you still there?"

9
"Cognito"

"Still here," he said as a knock on the door alerted me that the room service had arrived. I got up from the bed where I had relaxed to tell Mark about my journey thus far.

"You going to keep me updated on this adventure aren't you?" Mark asked.

"To keep my sanity; yeah."

"*Go to the center*... That has some interesting mind-body connotations," Mark added. "Especially with regards to our two year focus on the intelligence of the heart."

"Now you're talking. That's what I needed to learn I think. And knowing Mark, my good buddy, might help me figure out some meaning for all the stuff I went through yesterday, I thought I'd share."

I opened the door and motioned for the room service delivery person to come in, pointed to the desk, and slipped him a British five pound note. "Thanks," I whispered.

"What?"

"Just thanking room service," I answered. "Haven't eaten. Soooo... You think the story a bit strange?"

"Normal... that is, since you are the main character. For anyone else I'd be a bit concerned. Remember that Hopi Indian Reservation thing?"

"Yeah. The sweat lodge vision. Came true didn't it?"

Mark was really enjoying this. "Well, in a twisted way. You better eat your fish so it can '*goooo to dee center*'" he laughed. "Give me a call when you get to Ilfracombe. And relax! Try to enjoy yourself!" he added in final counsel.

"Roger that. *Cognito ergo sum*..." I said with another expression of thanks for being such a good friend to me.

I was eager to savor this North Atlantic halibut and spongy English style fries. I dove in to the hot food and then into a warm bed.

As I pulled the covers back, I also opened up my Bible for a quick verse which, in a superstitious sort of way, had become a habit; one I didn't especially want to ignore this night. I let it fall open to a page and then sat it beside me while I finished processing how I got here.

I smiled thinking about Mark Kastleman's serious side but also his friendship and understanding of the science called "mind/body" – the study of biological reactions to thoughts and emotions. This was Mark's strength and his recognition for it was growing rapidly.

Cognito Ergo Sum, I thought with a chuckle. Mark and I have debated a meaning behind that Latin expression for years. Now we both found that modern science was confirming our suspicions that quite possibly the opposite was true.

The Latin axiom, put forth as a more famous moniker by the father of modern science in medicine, the 17th century René Descarte, suggested that you had to prove such things as the soul's existence, scientifically, for it to be real; that empirical evidence is mandatory for a belief to graduate from theory to absolute truth.

Dealing with words and inspirational storytelling was my strength. Together Mark and I made a splendid team, if we could just figure out how to combine our two strengths and passions into one package.*

Cognito Ergo Sum, I thought to myself. *Descarte was wrong*, I added in reflection. Mark and I both allowed for science and its "seeing is believing" double-blind studies, but not to the exclusion of the unseeing power of instinct, faith, belief in something more than Descarte's Latin, which translated to English is, *"I think, therefore I am."*

If we could figure out how to combine the known and growing science surrounding the amazing powers of the brain, with emerging science of the intuitive and intelligent heart, we figured we would finally have a basis for working our writing and speaking into a new delivery format for self-improvement and inspiration.

"Sum," I muttered. "I am," I added as my eyes grew heavier. *Sum comes first. Cognito second… Sum Ergo Cognito…*

These were the last thoughts I pondered upon as the Bible sat open beside me, but not yet read. I forced myself to focus, pulled the book and page I let fall open up to sleepy eyes, and scanned it for some meaning.

I couldn't help chuckling as I read. I now knew all things would turn out for the best and that I was in the right place at the right time.

I flipped the lights out in the room, and finally also in my mind. I slipped into a well deserved state of sub-consciousness which never failed to invite other actors to the stage. Perhaps even pretty Alice would appear in a night of recuperative sleep where I could visit "dee center," and with her, chase the rabbit and his timepiece.

The verse I had just read from the wisdom of King Solomon now ran through my darkening mind:

"As a man thinketh…in his heart, so is he."

ACT II

EX NIHILO NIHIL FIT

"Nothing Comes From Nothing"

10
FINDING ILFRACOMBE

I cancelled the Hertz rental car when I saw where the driver sat. I'd seen enough James Bond movies to know that the Brits liked sitting in the passenger seat when they drove. Driving on the left side of the road was an added recipe for disaster.

I decided to let a train engineer drive me to Devon, in southwest England. I found it a pleasant and relaxing day of travel through the lush green English countryside. The rail line ended in Burnstaple just twenty miles south of my destination. I arrived at Ilfracombe late in the afternoon by bus. I am now ready to get down to some serious enjoyment of a traditional English dinner served here at the Bath House Hotel.*

☙❧

It was nearing the end of my first official day of writer's vacation. Having jotted a few notes in my journal, I now wanted to experience the hospitality of the Victorian era hotel and its restaurant. I entered the elegantly appointed dining room with its vintage furnishings covering more than one hundred years of history. I was quickly and politely seated at a small table near a gathering of costumed revelers enjoying the late afternoon "tea time" in a sectioned off area of the restaurant.

"My name is Jim. I hope this is suitable sir," a youthful waiter immediately offered.

"Quite nice, Jim," I answered with a smile. "I am James Pratt. Go by James."

He nodded politely.

"Is there a play in town?" I asked, as Jim the waiter held out a menu.

"Sir?" he answered.

"A play… You know; a theatrical production? I noticed some costumed looking folks in the area off to our left." I gestured with a nod in their direction.

"Oh that! Well, I should say that those must be the ghosts of Runnacleave," he chuckled. "You must be familiar with some of our legends and such. You aren't from these parts?" he inquired cheerfully.

I returned his question with a quizzical expression, wondering if I had slipped somehow into a proper British accent. "You can tell?" I finally answered with a smile.

"Actually sir, you must be from the western United States. I enjoy theatre myself and have studied the various forms of pronunciation of the King's language."

"You got it right, Jim. Californian, and a recent transplant to the Commonwealth of Virginia. So," I asked, "you are a drama lover? How nice. I do a bit of it myself."

"Acting?"

"Poorly. I write."

"Plays?"

"Novels."

"Any I might know?"

"*The Lighthouse Keeper* has done well here in the UK. *The Last Valentine* as well."

"Hum. I'm sorry to say, sir – I haven't heard of them. You are a guest of our hotel?"

"Yes," I said, eyes searching the menu.

"Very well. May I offer you a beverage while you decide?"

"Yes. Thank you. Water will do nicely."

"Very good," he answered as he left for the kitchen.

I turned my head and noticed the party of theatrical players, resembling turn-of-the-twentieth century residents, had dwindled in numbers. As I pursued the menu my eyes caught hold of the historical piece at the top of the first menu page. It read:

The friendly ambience of this hotel in Ilfracombe, North Devon, is part of what used to be known as the Runnacleave Hotel. The Runnacleave Hotel was very popular among the Victorians with the Tunnels Beaches opposite. Those with eyes for the unusual and keen imaginations may notice things about our Victorian heritage that others would miss. From all of us at the Bath House Hotel, a very good welcome whether you are here to enjoy our fine dining experience or are staying on as hotel guests.

Those with eyes for the unusual and keen imaginations… I muttered to myself as I re-read the historical vignette.

"Sir?" the waiter answered. Lost in thought, I hadn't seen him approach my table.

"Oh yes. Well, I was just saying that I like this place already. Those costumed folks are no doubt regulars and part of the 'set up' for ambiance. Smashing," I quipped, taking a stab at the British idiomatic expression.

I watched to see if the young man had a response. He merely creased his lips with a polite smile and said, "Very good, sir. Here you are." He poured from an ancient style bottle into the glass before me. "May I suggest some favorites?"

"Certainly," I replied.

"The game hen is particularly good. We serve it with your choice of potatoes, steamed greens, pudding or with the cottage pie."

"Cottage pie?"

"Yes." He pointed to the menu.

I pondered for a long minute as the waiter stood patiently by. "I'll go with your recommendations," I finally said, closing the menu.

"Very well. I shall bring our special of today; the game hen, pudding, steamed vegetables. If you should like coffee or tea I would be happy to provide your choice of several specialties."

I shook my head. "That won't be necessary, but thank you very much, Jim."

Jim evidently was cooking the meal himself, as quite a bit of time passed. My mind had been pleasantly away from the present moment as I watched the costumed diners from another era come and go, and finally disappear altogether. I was awakened from this reverie by another voice, this time female.

"Sir? Welcome to our restaurant. May I offer you the menu?"

"Oh, no. That won't be necessary. I've ordered, but something must have happened to Jim. He's been gone for quite awhile now."

Her face spoke of complete bewilderment. "I... I am not sure I follow, sir. Jim?"

"The waiter. The young man who took my order, thirty minutes or so ago."

The young lady shook her head, blinked several times, trying to comprehend, the way a confused person does.

"Let me help out here. If Jim hasn't already, please let the kitchen know I'd be interested in your 'dinner special.' The game hen?"

"Yes sir. Right away." I watched her as she shook her head, muttered something inaudible and disappeared into the kitchen.

Probably new, I thought as I examined the fine china tea cup sitting on a platter before me. *Tea time,* my mind next tuned in to. I raised the dainty cup and tried balancing it between my fingers as I imagined a cultured English gentleman might. I didn't notice him approaching.

"Here you are, sir," Jim suddenly announced. "I hope it suits your tastes. Will there be anything more?"

"Uh, Jim," I answered. "It's been some time since I ordered."

"Oh – well, quite right. I was serving some of our guests, right over there. I thought you wouldn't mind."

I turned to see no one where the handsome turn-of-the-century costumed group had been. "There is no one there," I pointed out.

"Oh. Quite right. Tea time has ended."

"Are they regulars?" I asked.

"Oh yes. Notables from miles around come to discuss philosophy and listen to each other's theories about life and such. I am seeing the daughter of one local philosopher at the present moment," Jim added in a whisper. "Your food, sir. It is growing cold."

"Right. Well, give my regards to the acting company when they return," I said, as a new guest appeared in their place. "That tall, bearded fellow... Wearing the turban?" I pointed to the Sikh garbed man who now stood outside the dining room and appeared to be seen gazing in.

"Oh yes, he is..."

"Tell him he was right," I chuckled cutting Jim off in mid-sentence. "I found my way."

"Mr. Pratt, sir?" Jim asked with a puzzled expression.

"Oh, nothing. I'm just recalling a humorous moment at an airport from the other day."

He offered a confused acknowledgment with a tilt of the head and then said, "Very well, sir. If you require further attention please don't hesitate to ring this bell," he added, pointing to the tiny brass hand ringer on the serving tray.

I winked, nodded, said 'thanks' and began to enjoy a hearty plate of English potatoes, delicious game hen, and perfectly cooked cream pudding. I soon found myself satisfied and filled. I rang the bell.

"Yes sir?" the waitress promptly answered. "I, uh... Your food, sir. I am sorry. I was away at the storage room. Did someone bring it so soon? And those plates; how very strange..." she said as her voice trailed off.

"Jim," I answered with a smile.

"Well, uh. Alright then," she answered in bewilderment.

"You're new here, aren't you?"

"Somewhat, but this is very strange."

"Stranger than fiction?" I questioned with a smile.

No answer came, just a befuddled look.

"It was very satisfying. Please bill it to my room and here's a 'five,' for you and another for Jim," I said, slipping two US five dollar bills into her hand. "When you see Jim, tell him the dinner was marvelous."

She nodded and backed away without a reply.

"Poor dear," I mumbled. *Well, let's check out Ilfracombe shall we?* I offered to imaginary friends.

Just then my instinct called to me. Most people know the feeling. You sense someone is watching you. You slowly turn and find you are correct. The tall man dressed Sikh-style, stood off to my right at the exit from the restaurant leading to the back street. I did a 360 degree turn to see if he were staring at someone else, then looked back to him, but he had disappeared.

The rabbit with a stop watch will run by any minute, I chuckled. *Curiouser and curiouser…*

11

"It's A Small World…"

"…after all. It's a small world after all… It's a small, small world," I found myself humming, as the words to the famous Disneyland ride celebrating world cultures, coursed through my mind. *Wonder how Jeanne's doing?* I thought. *Disneyland, day two.*

It had been only this morning since I left a message letting her know I had arrived safely. Now I wanted to tell her what I was seeing as I walked along the ocean front in Ilfracombe, England. I pulled the cell phone from my coat pocket and dialed.

It rang four times and then the message came up – my voice. "You have reached the Pratt's. Please leave a message."

"Hi honey. Just me. Arrived safe by train to Barnstaple and then to Ilfracombe by bus. I'm at the Bath House Hotel. Used to be called the Runnacleave. I'll email you the contact information tonight. Hope you are safe. Please give me a call. Love you."

I placed the cell phone back in my pocket and thought about how I already knew this would not be the only trip I would take to this place. I had to bring Jeanne with me to see the beauty and enjoy the slowed pace of life that exists here.

The sun was setting over the broad expanse of the Atlantic and I was alone to my thoughts about research – the writing of the *Hampton of Devon* story – and easily going back in time to the Victorian era, which this quaint seaside town seemed totally immersed in.

The boardwalk was paved over cobblestone, no doubt repaired hundreds of times over as many years due to the harsh North Atlantic climate. The shops of Ilfracombe harbor were neat, quaint, and tidy. As the seabirds screeched overhead, the scene offered me a sense of the setting the mystery author of *Hampton of Devon* had captured.

I climbed the nearby heights called Hillsborough where British cannon once protected this harbor village. I sensed I was in the right place at the right time and stopped to linger and enjoy a red-orange fire sunset mixing with the cobalt blue where sea meets sky. The pleasant hypnotic crimson, mirrored against a silver shimmering sea, held me totally captive. To my right a fog bank was either growing or dissipating, as it hugged the cove just feet above the water.

So hauntingly beautiful and breath-taking, this was one of those rare moments, which as a romantic, I now wished I could share with my love. I was thus entranced and spellbound as I descended Hillsborough, so I didn't notice him when he approached, once finding myself back at the quay.

"Sir? Mr. Pratt?" I heard from behind me. I turned to see the waiter from the hotel restaurant with a bouquet of flowers in his hand, then noticed the floral shop behind him.

"Jim! What a surprise! Can't be for me. Who's the lucky girl?"

"Oh," he blushed. "She just arrived home from school and I hope to make an impression," he answered with charming shyness. "How are you enjoying our town thus far, sir?" he politely asked.

"I'm in love with it. I feel strangely at home," I added. "And this," I said with a sweeping hand gesture to the sea. I examined Jim's choice of attire. His choice of formal apparel and the quaint derby hat indicated he was obviously joining the group of people in Victorian dress who had earlier enjoyed their afternoon tea at the hotel restaurant.

"Well, you must be an Englishman at heart," he replied.

"Perhaps it's my heart telling me I have come home. My ancestors came from England. What do you think?" I probed.

"Mr. Singh, would agree," he said with a smile. "Well, I must be off. Good evening to you, Mr. Pratt. I hope you find what you are looking for," he said as he tipped his hat.

"Thank you, Jim," I politely answered. *Mr. Singh?* My mind went to the happy girl of mixed English and Indian ancestry I had gotten to know a couple of days ago in Lexington. I thought it strange – a voice sounded in my head that I was being clued into something that could help my quest. I turned and said, "Nice hat by the way. Say this Singh fellow…"

I stood there amazed to find he had simply vanished. This was becoming a bit surreal; the "…now Jim's here and now he isn't," phenomenon of twice in the past hour. I decided I might need to finish my walk and go back to the hotel for an early retirement.

I walked back along the quay's Front Street toward Tunnels Beach, the same way I had come. Few people were out. There was a chill in the air. The sun had entirely set and that is when I noticed the bending of the lights in the northern sky. *Aurora Borealis… Magnificent!*

Just past St. James Cathedral now, I approached Capstone, a rocky mound rising abruptly as another sentinel, half the height of Hillsborough, and overlooking the coastal waters just south of the placid and sheltered harbor. Here the waves beat upon the rocks and spelled danger for the unschooled in boating. Atop Capstone hill the British flag fluttered in an almost constant breeze to remind the residents and the world, this flag marks the end of the road to some and the beginning to others in this part of England.

I found myself drawn there, mesmerized by the light display as I climbed the path to the top. I lingered here admiring the view. I could see the harbor and quay that led to a dock for small water craft. There, pulling out for a romantic evening of row-boating on the smooth and iridescent waters of the bay was, who appeared to be, my young friend Jim. A young lady with dark hair and sun bonnet laughed as she enjoyed the gentle ride through friendly waters just fifty plus feet from shore. He appeared in control of the craft and for now the waters below seemed calm enough.

"Helloooo… Mr. Pratt!" he called with a wave from the row boat below.

"Helloooo… Jim," I returned loudly with hands cupped over my mouth.

"The Northern Lights," he called. "Aren't they marvelous?"

"Indeed!" I called back. "Who's the pretty young woman?" I teased.

I could see Jim explaining something to her, and she turned to wave in my direction. She too was dressed for the party, and I thought this was one smart young man. He was doing the romance routine in an old fashioned, and undeniably winning, way.

"Mr. Pratt!" he called. "Meet Miriam!"

1 2
BREAKING THE FOG

Miriam! my mind spoke in silent over-drive.

I couldn't even begin to utter a response as the boat drifted into the low covering shroud of fog which had suddenly moved into the bay. As the fog swallowed the tiny craft I called to my new friend to be careful. There was no reply. The entire incident began to unnerve me.

This young man had so suddenly appeared in my life, and now a mere three to four hours later, I felt I had known him forever. I realized I might need some added sleep to clear the mental traveler's cobwebs. I entertained, for just seconds, that this might be one more dream from which I would soon enough wake up from. But I certainly know the difference, and the dream-like qualities I sometimes experience while awake are as normal for me in my novelist wanderings of the imagination as they would be weird for someone else.

I was sure Jim, as a local, was familiar with these bay waters, fog that suddenly appears, and any other dangers that might lurk a stone's throw from shore. I assumed I could ask him more about the town, about his life, tomorrow; and more about the strange coincidence of the second Miriam – namesake to the mystery author's heroin – to appear in my life in as many days.

The Disney tune re-visited my heart as I walked slowly back to the hotel. I made my way to my room and, while deep in thought about my reasons for coming here, dressed for sleep and flipped off the lights; an end to my first full day in Ilfracombe.

Like the fog shrouding the harbor and causing Jim and Miriam to disappear, I pulled the bed covers over me to sleep this off; make it go away so I could start with a fresh perspective tomorrow. I felt I had not just traveled across the sea, but to a time distant from my 2007 pace. The cell phone sat on the nightstand next to the Bible, which by habit, I had earlier placed there. Just one return call from Jeanne would keep me in touch with reality.

I tossed in an attempt to drift into *Never Land* but the nagging voice ringing inside my head wouldn't allow it. "Okay, one verse," I muttered as I flipped the light back on and allowed the bible to fall open. I pulled it up to my eyes and read words from the tireless ancient teacher and Apostle Paul, speaking to Corinthians.

"For now we see through a glass darkly; but then face to face: now I know in part; but then shall I know even as also I am known."

13
"Ex Nihilo Nihil Fit"

I awoke to a note under my door in answer to a request I had made the day before to the hotel concierge. It concerned finding a bicycle shop offering day rentals. I wished to see the town on wheels; not from the driver's seat of a car. That way I could stop, park it, wander in and out of shops, or take a ride into the countryside.

I was eager to locate a quieter residence for my stay – a Bed and Breakfast perhaps – and had a list of three known to provide the charm and atmosphere my writing and research might be inspired by. Besides, I find in old homes a certain character of the past residents, a ghostly history of sorts, which in my frame of mind would seem rather fitting.

The concierge was kind enough to give me the address of the nearest bicycle shop and recommended I get there early, just in case other tourists got the best pick of available two wheeled transports.

I wondered if I should linger for breakfast. I was eager to know that Jim and Miriam had made it back safely to the quay from their romantic boating interlude. I sensed the two had a story in them which I thought might serve as a good model for Hampton and Miriam of the story I was seeking to know more about. It would also be nice to have the friendly assistance in getting to know their home town.

I hurried and dressed, made my way to the lobby and peeked a glance inside the restaurant. The waitress from the evening before saw me and I was about to ask her if she had seen Jim, when she hurriedly turned her back and in nervous step disappeared into the kitchen area. *I'll ask for Jim at the front desk.*

I turned to head toward the front desk and stopped in my tracks at the sight of a man I had noticed from the evening before. The turban wearing Sikh – dagger and all, stopped in the ante-room, gazed in my direction, offered a slight nod of recognition, and then vanished into the street.

I stepped outside the hotel, only to find him gone. I searched up and down the street with no luck. I poked my head into the tunnel carved through a hill leading to Tunnels Beach. The Indian connection, which began at JFK, seemed to have a karma connection as well. Here too, I wondered if these "Sikh sightings" meant anything more than an over-active imagination on my part. *But then*, I quietly reasoned, *over-active is the best state to be in for my writing. Think I'll get that bike. Can ask about Jim when I check-out.*

I pulled my cell phone out of my pocket, excited to finally hear it ring. "Honey? That you?" Jeanne answered. "Where you been?" It was 10:00 pm in California as I let her know I had left two messages – one the day of my arrival in London, and one yesterday when I arrived in Ilfracombe – to which she answered she had not received either.*

"Well I didn't receive a message either day. Anyway… all well and we are having fun," she said.

"Hum... my mobile phone back home does that occasionally. I get a message the next day sometimes. Must have something to do with atmospheric interference. If you don't hear from me, just know I will check in. Give it some time before you worry too much. And keep having fun." She let me know she loved me, and I promised her a trip here next year.

"Hey, before I let you go... I mean it... You have to see this place Jeanne. It's like stepping back in time!" I next expressed my amazement for the Northern Lights. "I have never seen anything so spectacular! It is too awesome to see alone. You've got to be here with me when they show again. Like a curtain woven with threads of red, crimson, gold, silver, mixed against a palette of blended blues; an azure sky shimmering, moving, twisting, bending, melting in to the darkening Atlantic. I can't even do it justice with words."

She yawned, and said, "That's nice."

We signed off with, what for most are, the obligatory *"I love yous."* There was a time where I might have felt that way, but any expression of affection was now no pretense at all. I'd never been happier than at this stage of our life together, and I hoped she knew how genuine that feeling was as I said "goodbye."

I was well on to my rendezvous with a rental bike now, and came to the spot along the quay were I last had seen my young friends from the evening before, along with the spectacular light show. It felt good to be here and drink in the salty moist air of the southwest coast of my ancestor's homeland.

I thought about that now, along with the bible verse from last night. I occasionally looked down to the note in my hand, following the directions the concierge had meticulously created for me.

But as usual, no matter what task I am engaged in, my ponderings upon story lines, meanings, and where I am headed with writing are as deeply etched into my thought processing, as were the cobblestone grooves I now walked upon. Time had made these joints between individual stones deeper. And so, time had created in me a profound habit of always setting up a storyline, whether shopping for groceries, or looking for this bike shop, as I now was attempting to focus my attention upon.

I pondered upon how my family was linked to this land, its language and customs, as I made my way. *Perhaps there is more,* I thought, *to being here than simply researching for this forgotten author's story.* As it is for many Americans, this is the "homeland" for my paternal family line. A British Army Lieutenant, William Pratt had actually immigrated to the Americas in the 1630's, married a daughter of original Mayflower pilgrims, and ultimately started the Pratt saga from Massachusetts, to Connecticut, and finally west as far as California in the mid-1800's. I had to admit, having this knowledge about my heritage influenced me in many ways, not the least of which was to honor my ancestors and my inherited surname.

I decided that I would do all I could to immerse myself in the quaintness of this coastal region of England. I would become, for thirty days, a "subject of the Crown," and seek to understand my British heritage just as if my family had never left the motherland four centuries ago.*

Knowing your ancestry gives a person a sense of belonging and meaning; a connection to forbearers with dreams. Just as I would relish this opportunity to muse upon my roots, I needed to remember the purpose of my travel was in search for another man's family history as well. What his name was, I didn't know. What his skills were, included creative writing and a romantic way of thought.

If I connected to whoever wrote *Hampton of Devon,* I would understand his "ghost writing" whispers; I'd get the remainder of his tale, I determined.

I looked up to find myself at the end of Broad Street facing the harbor. I had missed a turn. I searched for the sign posts, examined the notes for the bike shop location, and now had to backtrack. I plotted a bit more carefully and decided to study what was in front of me at eye level, and not street level.

I proceeded back two blocks, passing the Prince of Wales and George and Dragon pubs, and then turned up a narrow lane bordered by pleasant row houses on one side and the narrow Broad Street shops on the other.

I considered that this bike ride I was about to begin into the country would be good for me; for my sense of enjoyment in this hunt for a story. How I handled this research and investigation of the mystery writer's identity and his copyrights created a need to decide between two directions I could take. I could begin this quest the easy way, or my most often chosen method of attacking a challenge – swim against the current, but have a bit of fun at it too.

The easiest way to handle this search was to probe around town, spend time in the library, museum, become acquainted with the literature lovers here, and listen to their tales of the story weavers from days gone by, who had called this village "home."

If I hound-dogged those clues starting with the librarians, bookstore keepers, shop owners, adding an email campaign to college professors of 19th and early 20th century English literature, along with general nosing around, the *Hampton of Devon* story and his writer would, no doubt, emerge.

But where's the fun in starting that way? I was here for one month. I had time. In a week, two weeks, or even three, I could always do the "paper trail" thing.

I didn't want to work too hard; I wanted to play. Play to me is different than what my wife does – the connection to Disneyland, thrill rides, and beach parties. I enjoy hanging out in the past, seeing a place through someone else's eyes, enjoying the scenery, and meditating on the deep stuff mixed with a heavy dose of imagination.

The playing had already begun last night at dinner with the side-show of happy costumed "tea time" revelers. Then with the Aurora Borealis shimmering above a delightful young couple on a romantic boat ride through the ghostly low-lying fog, I found time standing still.

I paused, realizing I was caught up in reverie again, looked down at my notes, looked up at a sign on a post with a bicycle on it, and realized I must be near the rental store. I turned a corner and next to another small store was the shop with sign hanging over the entry door. "Singh Bicycle" it read. I entered the bicycle shop. It was quiet. I rang the bell at the counter. No one answered. An ancient looking bicycle, though in excellent condition, was propped up along the counter. A small white envelope with a hole punched in the upper right corner with a string looped though it, hung from the handle bars. I examined it. It was addressed in elegant cursive to, who else... *me*.

I slid the string-attached envelope off the handle bars assuming my reservation and invoice was enclosed, while I simultaneously thought, *No way am I taking this hunk of old metal without gears up and down these hills.* My mind easily went to the summer of 1962 and my first paper route in the hilly lanes called "the Knolls" at the east end of Simi Valley. I pushed that old bike more than peddled it and all for $22 dollars for three months work too.*

I was curious about the contents of the envelope though. My thumb and index finger felt something hard, flat, yet round inside. I opened it, allowing a coin to fall into my hands. I took out a note on yellowed onion skin paper. In a curious eastern style handwriting it read:

"Mr. Pratt. You will be wanting to take the bicycle up the hill along the Granville Road until Torrs Walk. A road will appear that is not on a city map where Torrs Walk ends. An unpaved lane, it will lead you to a pleasant cottage. This lane is called Lamp Hill by the landowner. This token shall identify you at the gate. Harjot."

"Harjot?" I wondered if it were some English expression I had yet to become familiar with. Obviously the owner of the shop knew my name and must have had something unexpected come up. I stuck the note in my pocket but had a better idea. I would take a cab. I could always come back for the bike. That way if something was amiss in this odd arrangement I could get back into town easily.

I then made a close examination of the medallion in question. I flipped it over, and over. The engraved words seemed familiar. Since learning Spanish as a young man in South America, and then as the Hispanic population boomed back home in Los Angeles, I had toyed with the other romantic languages, including Latin.

One side read "EX TEMPORE" engraved in a semi-circle fashion on the upper edge of the copper coin. An engraved profile of a man's head, Romanesque in nature, was centered in the coin with rays of sunlight engraved behind it. The Latin, "EX ANIMO," was engraved below the silhouette on both sides with a date in Roman numerals, MCMXII. On the bottom edge appeared "Power."

"I know these words," I voiced. Excitedly I flipped the medallion over to see the word "Thought" engraved with another Latin expression was engraved on the top edge.

"EX NIHILO NIHIL FIT!" I breathed aloud. I was becoming a bit excited. I strained, as my mind worked on the complete meaning.

I put aside my idea of calling a cab. My hands trembled as I safely deposited the coin inside a zipper pouch of the light parka I was wearing. I reached for the handle bars and everything sped up for me.

My mind raced at the exhilaration of this connection so early in my serendipitous search for the meaning behind an obscure document, written a century before by an unknown writer in this town. I had learned years ago that when a person sends an expectation out into the world, the Universe begins to respond in the most sudden and strange ways.

I walked the exquisitely restored turn-of-the-century bicycle out the shop door. I noticed no one as I exited down the narrow passageway, Albert Court, to the street below, though early morning walkers and tourists certainly began to fill the streets. My mind was focused laser like as my brain sorted through a thousand memory files.*

"Ex Nihilo Nihil Fit…" I posed silently as I clambered aboard the old bike and wobbled a bit to steady it. Its meaning was becoming clearer.

I pushed my fifty-something legs into action and felt like the nine year-old kid on the first day of my newspaper adventure in the summer of 1962. I was sure good things were in store for me then, among the hills and dirt lanes of the rocky Knolls in my hometown. I peddled toward my destiny at Lamp Hill Lane computing the Roman numeral on the back side of the coin. *1912*, I determined.

I felt it almost effortless to climb Granville Road as my excitement and anticipation grew with each turn of the chain on the single sprocket vintage bike from circa 1910. *Jeanne should see me*, I thought.

I reached the crest of Granville Road, stopped and looked down at the bay behind me, exultant at this start to my first day of work. The bright blue sea west led to home, but I wouldn't return until I had my answers. I coasted before climbing again on Torrs. I smiled as I thought of the meaning behind the Latin, "Ex Nihilo Nihil Fit."

Truly, I reminded myself, "*Nothing comes from nothing.*"

14
TOKEN TO ANOTHER SIDE

Just like the coin, there are two sides to places, people, and perspectives. I was seeing another side of England, life, and how things appeared to really be for most British outside of major cities like London.

Ilfracombe is an idyllic, charming, seaside town with classic Victorian storefronts on High Street in the city center to modern town homes sprinkled among centuries old row houses and cottages. Walking the length and breath of the town is a thirty minute exercise. You sense a separation from a greater, busier world, as well as a connectedness of those living with those gone before. This quieter world is as different from my fast pace in the US as the two sides of this coin with its messages; both sides offered differing values.

I was left to ponder upon these Latin meanings and link to the two words which had appeared in the website address during my online hunt for *Hampton of Devon* as I pushed the bike peddles. This odd token supplied to me by the vintage bike renter was sparking creativity in me, yet he could not know of my purposes for traveling five thousand miles from home.

It was all so synchronistic, like one more clue to yet another piece of my puzzle offered me, but still the pieces still didn't make that much sense. I felt in my parka to see if the coin was actually there, or if I had again allowed imagination to get the better part of me.

I stopped my bicycle ride to catch my breath and to take in the view after climbing the hill. The harbor village below boasted of craggy cliffs and rolling hills which extend up from the seashore made of rocky coves linked to long stretches of course beach. I was above it all now; breathing the scene in and feeling far away from cares – a world of speed and demands. After having gone through so much exhausting adventures trying to get out of the States, I now was glad I had not turned back and gone home. I felt if I could have many days such as this I might actually regain youthful vigor and health.

I continued to ponder upon the magical words of the coin given me by a stranger and to be used for entry to another side of some gate I was now on the hunt for. I found myself so engaged in thought as I reached the end of Torrs Walk. I reached for the note stuffed in my windbreaker pocket with my cell phone when the phone rang.

"Hello?" I answered. "Darn!" I added, fumbling with the cell phone and missing the call. I looked for a sender's number to register on the screen as I balanced the antique bike between my legs. Nothing came up. "Jeanne or Mark," I allowed in self-speak. *Well, they'll leave a message*, I determined as I stuck the phone into my trouser pocket.

"Okay dirt lane. Appear," I commanded as my eyes scanned the rolling hills off to my right and toward the ocean. I peddled a bit more and then what did finally appear was a trail that showed, what looked like, wheel ruts of some kind grown over by grasses. "Nothing here," I breathed as I looked up its serpentine path bordered by vine covered stone walls. The country lane was entered through bordering trees, reaching to connect to one another in a tunnel-like manner. A time and weather-beaten sign, perhaps fifty years old read: "Unsuitable for Motor Vehicles."*

It was certainly not what I expected to find in searching for the obscure Lamp Hill Lane on the bike shop owner's note. I had come this far and determined to at least see the ocean from the crest of the hill where it appeared this lane finally ended.

Just then I heard the sound of the cell phone indicating a message had been left. I reached into my trouser pocket, pulled it out, hit "play message," and listened. It was Mark.

"Hey, Jimmy boy. Where you been? Tried reaching you in London at your hotel after you called today. I found some information that might be of interest to…" then it went dead.

"Called today?" I mumbled. I looked at the time and date the message was sent. "Two days ago?" These cell phones were definitely suffering from slow cyberspace connections. I reminded myself to call Mark back when I returned to the hotel this afternoon and continued on.

I walked the bike up the pleasant wheel-rutted lane, and noted grazing sheep with pastures on either side. I wondered what kind of vehicle had caused these ruts, since motor vehicles were unadvised.

Up hill, the ocean was obscured from my view but the scent of salty sea air filled my lungs as I enjoyed the pleasant bike-pushing walk, and let my imagination go to play.

I wondered who might have lived here when these walls were placed on either side. I envisioned children at play, a carriage coming up this hill, and wished for the time I had never known; a place and world where people answered calls, because someone was close enough to voice one to them. I missed that age in which mail was stamped, and to receive a letter was a treat; even a special occasion. I wondered how it might have been without the modern conveniences and thought upon the task of writing a manuscript without the aid of a computer, one hundred years ago.

Every word placed upon precious paper with ink pen would be carefully thought out; no "white out" and no cut, paste, or delete keys to make quick work of typos and poorly structured sentences. The author would be a master at words as much out of shear necessity as he would from developed talent.

I hardly felt the time slip by as I stopped, looked back and realized I had reached the crest and a gate. The gate, at approximately my height, could be walked around, though bolted and locked about a post with a chain and key lock that appeared twice my age.

I searched for a house, as the crest of this hill leading to the coastal view of ocean and beaches was within two to three hundred yards distant. I must have already walked that distance from the last paved street in Ilfracombe. I took the bike off the lane and scooted it around the iron gate with the intent of walking it up the hill to look for the mysterious house the note had led me to believe existed here.

No sooner did I pick the bike up to carry it around the gate through tall field grasses than I found myself stepping in a rut, losing my balance, and falling forward. Bike on top me, and a little twinge of pain to my right ankle, I arose and began to brush myself off. I felt for my cell phone and then looked to the gravel below my feet. It had fallen from my pocket. As I reached down to pick it up, new elements caught me by surprise.

"Now this is really weird," I let out to no one. This side of the gate was a perfectly groomed, though wheel rutted, unlike the uncared for road on the side of the gate where I had come from below. I turned a complete 360 degrees and found myself in a well-cared for plot of land on this sea-side of the iron gate.

Picking the bike up, I noticed something else. The coin given me by the bike shop owner had fallen from my pocket and tumbled into the tall grass exactly on the border of the gate post. I immediately leaned the bike up against the gate and stepped one foot on either side searching the tall grass for several minutes, but was unable to find it.

Well, maybe on my way out, I determined. I picked up where I left off and reached for the bike when I became aware of a horse drawn carriage making its way over the crest of the hill in the distance. "We'll be right back to the Twilight Zone after these messages from our sponsor," I voiced aloud as I froze, amazed at what was approaching.

"Hello, Mr. Pratt," a deep but pleasant accented voiced greeted me as the driver brought the carriage to a halt. "You are Mr. Pratt, are you not?"

"Last time I checked. Of course I could be someone else. That happens in dreams sometimes," I answered. "You... You sir, are the fellow from the Bath House Hotel? The man with the costume party yesterday. I pointed you out to the waiter. I mean you are dressed..."

"As a Sikh of the late nineteenth century?"

"Well, that would be my guess. But why? I mean are you with the bike shop? I got this invitation, and..." I stopped and reached for the crumpled note in my trousers. "I expected..."

"Not a Sikh," he kindly interjected, "and not a horse and carriage."

"Well, I don't know what I expected."

"I am known to many as simply 'Singh' and I own the bicycle shop in Ilfracombe. The horse you see here has been replaced by that more modern means of travel," he said nodding toward the bike, "...and automobiles, I'm afraid. Please allow me," he voiced as he came down from the carriage and picked the bike up and placed it in the back seat. "Won't you join me?" he asked, as he motioned to the seat next to the driver's.

I limped around the front. "Nice horsey," I said as I patted him on the nose.

"You have injured your leg, Mr. Pratt?"

"Oh, just a twisted ankle. I tripped walking around the gate. It will pass," I said climbing aboard.

"The medallion?" he asked.

"Oh yes. That was also a casualty of the fall. It slipped out of my pocket as I fell. I searched but didn't find it. But, I assure you, I am James Pratt."

"Well then, perhaps we will find it later. You could not have come thus far were it not so. Let us show you the grounds." He spoke to the horse, tapped its back with the reins, and pulled the carriage about.

We easily climbed the remainder of the hill, and there before me on the other side upon a leveled plot of ground, was the most delightful picture-book cottage one might hope to find in all of England. As different from the village I had just left behind, on this side of the gate, as Ilfracombe was from London.

Could not have come thus far... were it not so... I repeated over and over. *Strange,* I allowed silently, in reference to the lost medallion. I said nothing as we came to a halt in front of the gate. A waist high rock wall surrounded the home. From the gate a neat path of cobblestone pavers led to the stoop and entry door. On either side of the path a wide variety of perennials greeted the eye. The profusion of colors was enchanting enough, but raked earth paths meandered off the main walkway bordered by roses, small shrubs, with neatly cut lawn interspersed between.

I gazed off to my right to witness the vastness of the Atlantic and could see the last roof lines in the town of Ilfracombe nestled among the hills far below and to the north. "I didn't realize how far I had come," I said, as Singh unhitched the horse and led him to a nearby stable.

"Yes, Mr. Pratt. You have come a long way," he said with a smile. "A very long way, indeed."

As I waited for Mr. Singh to return, I enjoyed something I rarely slowed down enough to notice. Small creatures called this garden home. A butterfly fluttered about. Bees enjoyed the nectar from the flowers. A squirrel scampered across the path to the house and clambered up a young oak. I slowed my breathing and felt rested, losing track of any time as the calming influence of this pleasant oasis, with the sea bordering one side, and countryside of rolling hills and verdant grasses bordering the other.

"How do you feel, Mr. Pratt?" Singh's baritone voice interrupted.

"I feel wonderful," I returned. "This is so…"

"Peaceful?" Singh asked, then pointed to my foot.

"Hum. No pain. Nothing. Gone. How nice."

He nodded, smiled, and gestured toward the cottage entry door. "Well then. Shall I be welcoming you to our hide-a-away?"

I nodded and followed.

"Oh. I must insist," he said turning to me as we reached the door. "Would you be so kind to keep this medallion with you at all times?" He held out a duplicate of the one I had just lost.

My mind questioned him for a moment, but then thought, *Why not?*

Mr. Singh held the door open.

I entered another world.

15
Hyde And Sikh

The house was simple but of tasteful antique décor with nothing appearing newer than a copy of Robert Lewis Stevenson's *Treasure Island,* which sat upon a shelf along with other works of notable English writers.

"May I?" I asked.

"Certainly," Mr. Singh replied. "If you will excuse me, Mr. Pratt. I shall notify my master of your arrival."

I nodded but was already engrossed in the title page and inked entry which read:

For a young and aspiring writer. May grace follow you in your noble yearnings to pen the morals which fill your heart.
Robert Lewis Stevenson, London 1884.

"A first edition autographed copy," I whispered in amazement. I carefully replaced the book upon the shelf. "Kipling," I said as I reached for *The Man Who Would Be King.* I again opened to the title page, but with an almost reverence, and this time read:

With warm regards for a talented thinker.
Rudyard Kipling, 1888.

My eyes continued to scan the titles found upon the entry hall book shelf. There was Victor Hugo's *Les Miserable,* Poetry of Walt Whitman, Elizabeth Barrett Browning, and a copy of Tolstoys' *War and Peace,* and the list went on.

"My master wishes to welcome you to tea," Singh declared, breaking me from my reverie.

"His books," I said. "These rare editions are a treasure beyond anything I have ever seen. Your master is a collector, Mr. Singh?"

He smiled but did not answer.

My mind continued wandering the pages of each book I had religiously handled. "Amazing," I declared under my breath as Singh's voice pulled me reluctantly away from this sacred spot of rare collectables. "I love original editions," I added.

"If you please," my new turban wearing friend in Indian attire said, while gesturing with his hand toward a sunny patio through yet another set of window dressed double doors.

I glanced off to my right and noticed a modest kitchen with dining table and chairs, a center cutting board, hand pump water spout and sink, and pot belly style stove, but noticed no modern appliances whatever. *Odd,* I mused.

I stopped and looked to my left which opened to a pleasant sitting room with aged but apparently restored furnishings, and beyond I discerned at least two other rooms; bedrooms I supposed. We quickly exited to find a delightful rear patio surrounded by shrubs, lawn, perennials, and bordered by waist-high hedge shrubbery. A gate led from this enclosed area and I could see a pleasing vegetable garden with the ocean in full view beyond. The land had crested and now a gentle downward slope met the Atlantic's western horizon, and what I knew would be Ireland beyond; to the north the Welsh coast and Bristol Bay.

I drank deeply from the sea breeze, scented with the prolific chrysanthemum, and then took a seat on a wicker chair set at an outdoor table of simple pine, built to seat four. My hand moved along the edges of the elegantly designed border.

"A fine piece of woodwork," I said.

"My master enjoys working with his hands," Singh answered.

"Reminds me of my Dad's old wood shop in Idaho," I voiced. "He was meticulous, as the author of this piece of furniture obviously is."

"Author?" Singh voiced. "Strange you should use that term."

"Guess it's the writer in me admiring the art form of another," I returned.

Spread upon the table was a setting for two, a basket with fruit, and a tea kettle with cups, and what I assumed were crackers of some sort. "Tea time?"

"If you desire," Singh returned as he took my cup and brought the kettle to it.

As he poured a cup of tea I inquired, "You have referred to the home owner as 'my Master' with every reference to the owner. From the note directing me here I had assumed that this was your home. I must be missing something in translation... Thank you," I finished as he poured the yellow looking beverage to the rim of a delicate tea cup.

"Sugar?" he asked.

"Please," I answered.

"One lump. Two?"

Those look like rock candy and mighty big lumps, I thought. "One, thank you," I replied.

"May I join you for tea?" he asked.

"Of course! I am a bit off as far as tea time customs go."

He poured himself a cup and waited for me to taste first.

"This... this, is... unique," I offered. "Herbal?'

"Chrysanthemum, to be exact. We dry them and use them for tea as is custom in East Asia. Good for fevers, ailments, but as a general tonic, quite beneficial."

"Hum. I'll have to look into that at the health food store back home," I offered as I gazed upon my pleasant surroundings. "A bit of heaven you have carved out here, Mr. Singh. I am to take it you have invited me here to show me your Bed and Breakfast? Well, I must say I'm delighted, impressed, and congratulate you."

"Bed and Breakfast? Well, I have never heard my master's retreat spoken of in that way."

"Oh. I didn't mean to offend, I simply..."

"No offense taken," the well-mannered Indian replied. "I noticed you yesterday at the Runnacleave Hotel after our regular afternoon social gathering... Just a few fellow philosophers. I made an inquiry; from instinct. You see, Mr. Pratt, my master has been ill lately. He keeps to himself except for small amounts of writing accomplished between periods of rest. His wife has traveled to London to seek expert medical advice for his condition and I have agreed to look after him. I was informed by the concierge that you were interested in both a bicycle and a cottage atmosphere for your purposes of writing."

"I did ask the concierge, yes. You said 'Runnacleave Hotel'. I suppose you locals still call the Bath House Hotel by its former Victorian name?"

Singh simply blinked as if contemplating a response. "We socialize there, yes. A pleasant assortment of Indian, and Eastern Asia citizens along with English who now call Devon home, gather once each week to discuss culture and matters of truth. As I was saying, once I knew you were not only looking for a place to stay but are an American writer, my interest beset me and I inquired with my master regarding the possibility of offering you free room and board during your time here in Ilfracombe."

"Very thoughtful," I replied. I wasn't sure where this was headed, though I was enjoying the tea, the scenery and my second run-in with a Sikh in one week. My estimation for their kindness, directness, and subdued state of spiritual attitude impressed me; well except for the Avis rental return check-in cousin who insisted I had an imaginary fender bender added with, "...this wheel be costing you."

I waited to hear more about this sudden "free room" offer, but met silence from my dagger wearing friend instead. So I decided to probe the offer in my own way.

"Are you friends with a young man named Jim? The waiter at the... ah, Runnacleave?"

A sudden chill filled the space between us, and a marked look of sadness spoke volumes from his eyes. The proper and stoic Sikh turned his head. I could tell something had emotionally reached him with my simple question. He finally turned his dark but compassionate eyes toward me and spoke with reverence due a beloved, but long lost friend, "Yes. The lad and I are friends."

He sipped from his tea, as I did from mine, but now I kept my eyes set upon his body language. Something had disturbed him and I wanted to know what it could possibly be.

"I just met him yesterday. Could you tell me his last name?"

"Yesterday?" he said pausing. Then he shook his head.

"I met him at the hotel restaurant."

His voice was tender. "Hyde. It was James Hyde," he answered softly.

"Was?"

"Is, I suppose. Quite right. James Hyde it is," he added.

"I shall ask for him then, upon my return to the hotel. A fine young man. I last saw him in a row boat on the bay with a charming young lady."

"Miriam," he whispered.

"Yes!" I replied.

He stood and turned toward the ocean. It glistened in the mid-morning sunlight and I wondered what he might be thinking; what the mention of these two had caused him to stir so poignantly. After some silence I decided to break the ice.

"Do you always wear the dagger?" I asked.

"A devout Sikh would not be a true Sikh without his *kirpan*," he said as he slowly turned to face me.

"And turban? I understand you are not permitted to cut your hair?"

"It is one of the five ways."

"Interesting. So Harjot, per the note, is your first name and Singh your last?" I queried.

"Singh is not a surname as Pratt, or Stevenson, or Kipling. It is a name given to a family of believers. Thus, in Sikh ways, everyone may be a Singh."

"Does it have a meaning?"

"Lion," he simply answered.

"And Harjot?"

"God's Light," he again politely replied.

I sipped at the herbal tea, quite impressed with this man and his various devotions. De-votion to a mysterious estate owner, devoted to his work, friends, philosophy, faith, God…

"May I ask the name of the homeowner who you refer to as 'Master'?"

"Yes, you may," he said as he finished his tea. "But first I must ask of you regarding his offer. Have you an interest in this exchange?"

"Exchange?" I questioned.

"Forgive me. I quite forgot. My master is a writer who seeks the advice of a fellow writer, and when I informed him of a notable American novelist who had just come to Ilfracombe, he was delighted. He has asked if you would exchange the free stay here in his cottage for read-ing a page or two of his daily hand-written words."

"Editing work?" I asked.

"Considering your expertise, it would be most welcome," Harjot Singh answered.

"May I think on this? I must be getting back to my hotel room. I could call you from there?" I returned.

"You must have a very strong and formidable voice, Mr. Pratt," he chuckled.

This was the first hint of a sense of humor in the man, but I didn't see the humor in my question, so I asked, "As in a 'telephone call'?"

"An Alexander Graham Bell talking device?"

Now I was the one chuckling. "Yes, one of those."

"We neither have such a device nor electricity here. Is there a problem?"

"You mean, you have no electrical outlets?"

Harjot shook his head. "We have ample lighting with some of the finest smokeless lamps. We heat our rooms with smokeless hearths and have on hand an adequate supply of coal. But electrical amenities, there are none."

"Why?"

"Well, you see Mr. Pratt, this is remote, and of course we have just turned a century. Not all cities possess such advantages."

Turn of which century? I wondered in silence. I felt like a game of cat and mouse were in play here. I studied the man for any hint of pulling my leg, attempt at comedy, or some sort of sly ruse played upon a dumb American.

I stood, stretched, and gazed about me at the fabulous vista of countryside and ocean cre-ating such freshness and tranquility. I examined Harjot Singh. He stood there, an imposing figure of a man with squared shoulders, a regal attitude and posture as if a prince of India. His dagger bothered me a bit, but the man possessed no apparent guile, and I strangely trusted him. Yet… Something told me I was either missing an element to this offer, or this was a new twist to the weeklong experiment in strange traveling adventures; the inexplica-ble, sometimes dangerous, and oddly curious sort.

Never make a quick decision on an empty stomach, my father used to say. I determined to go back to the Bath House Hotel and "sleep on it." Besides, I wanted to find Jim Hyde, the vanishing waiter. Between him and my new friend Harjot, I began to have the feeling that this part of my literary motivated trip to find *Hampton of Devon's* writer would become known in my journal writings as, "Hyde and Sikh."

16
OUTER LIMITS

I continued sipping my tea and pondering my response to Harjot Singh. I imagined Vic Perrin, the "Control Voice" of the early 1960's television drama *Outer Limits*, walking through the garden gate any minute. I could almost hear his voice saying: *There is nothing wrong with your television set. Do not attempt to adjust the picture. We are controlling the transmission. We can reduce the focus to a soft blur, or sharpen it to crystal clarity. For the next hour, sit quietly and we will control all you see and hear...*

"Mr. Pratt?" Singh finally said, interrupting my television trivia reverie.

"Uh, yes…" I stammered. "I was lost in thought," I said apologetically.

"My master's offer? I was wondering if you might like to take some of his writings with you to your hotel before you return tomorrow to confirm or reject the terms of our offer for your room and board."

"Yes. Of course. I would love to take some writings with me."

"Very well. I shall go and retrieve a written invitation and a sample of my master's writing."

The offer was a strange one – way outside the limits of anything I might have imagined, even for this less-than-structured writing vacation. "Singh… Can I again ask the name of the proprietor of this pleasant estate?"

He had excused himself from the table and then faced me as I downed the remainder of the herbal tea. "Yes," he simply answered, then turned to enter the cottage for the papers.

I was enjoying this fanciful journey to another world, and wondered how I could have ever lived so many fast-paced years without exploring a land such as this one, with its unique characters and mystical qualities.

I stood, stretched, and moseyed over to the waist-high hedges separating this backyard patio from the vegetable garden. The garden was freshly hoed and weeded. I enjoyed the sight of late flowering peas, the scent of celery, the abundance of cabbage, carrots, and potatoes.

I shook my head free from the green-garden trance when a middle-aged man; bearded, full head of hair, but seemingly frail – opened the door to a sturdy stone-built tool shed, turned, and apparently began speaking. Obscured by the shady oak planted between the garden and the shed, I strained my eyes to focus, and my ears to listen in on the conversation between, who I assumed was, the home owner and Singh.

Failing to catch anything, and with both apparently having suddenly disappeared from the scene, I turned to face the house.

"Singh! How did you…"

The pleasant Sikh simply smiled, offered a respectful inclined nod of his head. "My master wishes to inform you that his offer includes one hour of light gardening and kitchen preparations each day. As I mentioned, he is quite frail, and as I must be about other business during the day, he and I would greatly appreciate your acceptance."

"Absolutely… that is once I sleep on this. I enjoy gardening very much, and fresh food is the best. I should be able to whip something up in the kitchen to surprise and satisfy."

"Whip up?" Singh asked.

"Throw together. Create. Invent."

"Oh," he said with a nod of understanding, but only for the appearance of courtesy. "Here are the pages I promised," Singh offered, extending a manila envelope with string ties at the flap. "I do hope you may enjoy my Master's writing. Also enclosed is a letter of explanation as to why he has chosen to remain aloof. I do hope you will understand. He extends his apologies in advance for not greeting you personally."

"I saw him back by the shed. With you I believe?"

"Yes. If my master is not at his home in the village below, he rests part of the day in the sunshine beyond the garden and the remainder in his bedroom here, with an adjoining study."

"Why don't we go and just say hello?" I asked, and moved toward the gate to the garden.

"Mr. Pratt… Stop! You must not go. Not now. The sun sets."

It's mid-day, I posed silently. *Stranger by the minute,* I thought. "Sure. No problem. Well, thanks for this," I said, holding up the envelope. "I'll just walk down the drive to where I left the bicycle," I added.

"That will not be necessary," Singh declared. "Your bicycle is in the carriage. You do not recall?"

I nodded thoughtfully.

"I will be driving you to the gate," he politely rejoined.

"I like to walk. Really. Why don't I just grab the bike from the back seat and…"

"I insist," he replied.

Something about his insistence gave me the impression that this was where I take his carriage and make my escape from *Fantasyland.*

"Very well," I finally replied as I followed him through the tidy home, and back to the front where the carriage had been parked. Singh quickly hitched up the sturdy looking sorrel and we were off to the front gate.

I thought there was *no way* I was coming back here except to return the papers I would edit tonight and thank Mr. Singh for the courtesy and offer. The tranquility and ambiance was refreshing but the "my Master" stuff and strangeness of the requirements was too much, even for an adventurer who loved losing himself in obscure settings and the past.

"Here we are, Mr. Pratt. Did you retain the coin I gave you earlier?"

"The replacement? Yes. Here it is," I said with a smile as I pulled it from my pocket.

"Please take care with that coin, Mr. Pratt. It is the last of its kind and is a link to a purpose my Master will be explaining. Have a very good evening. I look forward to our visit tomorrow."

"Quite," I replied with English manners and some sort of charm I hoped passed me off as just another gentleman from Devon. I quickly made for the bicycle and my escape. I was pleased to make it around the post to the other side of the gate and was suddenly struck by the lack of upkeep on this side. I meant to ask Singh about that, and I turned to do so now.

"Wow!" I allowed. Singh was once again a pro at coming and going at the speed of light compared to the slowness of the pace around the grounds I had just visited. I could barely see the tail end of the buggy as I strained my eyes towards the crest of the hill in the direction of the house. I couldn't believe what I was seeing! Singh wasn't fooling about what time of day it was, yet I had only been there an hour at best, to my reckoning.

The setting sun created a surreal picture of a black carriage silhouetted against it, as if the dark features of Singh's disappearing buggy was becoming swallowed in its resplendence. Vic Perrin's voice came to my mind as I watched Singh disappear:

> *You are about to experience the awesome mystery which reaches*
> *from the inner mind to... The Outer Limits!*

17
THE BOOK

It was indeed late afternoon as I coasted the bicycle back into Ilfracombe city limits proper. I decided to blow off my concern about the loss of time as one more occasion of being absolutely caught up in the moment. After all, the rare books, he beautiful estate, the peace and tranquility, the time it took to ride the bike, walk the bike, ride in a carriage twice…maybe I just wasn't paying attention.

So my second night in Ilfracombe was approaching. Yesterday was travel and getting to know the town. Today was a pleasant first full day of exploration, keeping me out of the city. This evening I was determined to get to know a bit of how people spent their time in this laid-back seaside resort town.

I looked forward to a hot shower, a hot meal, and a stroll downtown on "High Street." Like the Main Streets of home, it seems every English town has its High Street with its pubs, restaurants, bookstores, corner drug store, and novelty shops.

I easily found myself back at The Bath House Hotel, parked the bike, and made my way to my room after several "good days" from hotel staffers. As interesting and fun as my trip to Singh-Land had been, I felt relieved to be back in my comfort zone where the present reality and sanity collided to make me decide which minor irritation or stress of life to address first.

Showers work to help sort things out. I always get great ideas with hot water beating on my brain, so I checked that one off my list. Naps help and I found one hour in "Never Land" indeed was refreshing. Food calms me, but I had a duty to find out if my wife Jeanne had survived Disneyland and the sharks off the waters at Newport Beach. I called. No answer. Left a message and then decided I would continue to try if it took me all night. Check…

I dressed and found myself walking out the door when I noticed an envelope had been slipped underneath. "Hotel bill," I said, tossing it behind me on to the bed.

Exiting the hotel, I was determined to discover a first rate restaurant – a four star – offering a hot plate of English bred prime rib beef. Corned beef with cabbage would do as well, I considered.

In this food frame-of-mind I advanced toward High Street and away from the bay. I couldn't help but notice a sight that had entirely left my mind during the day but captured every part of me now, just as it had last evening. I felt myself drawn to this heavenly display and not back up the hill toward my planned destination of restaurant and book store hunting on Ilfracombe's main thoroughfare.

Drawn like a magnet, I soon stood where I had upon my first arrival here in Ilfracombe, just after having been treated to the hearty dinner at The Bath House Restaurant, by Jim Hyde.

The shimmering veil of last night, as if a thin silken shroud drawn to separate heaven from earth, appeared on stage to once again delight all citizens of this quiet seaside town. Like a curtain ready to open for the stage play, the celestial veil seemed to draw up until it left the bay a ghostly glowing body of prism-like qualities – rippling with countless shades of azure blue and amber-gold; platinum tinted white caps quaking, but not breaking. In a word, I was once again spellbound, lost to the reality of the present moment, and entirely forgetful of any hunger pangs created from a busy day away from here. With the last strands of curtain-like light hiding heaven's deeper secrets, the rainbow luminescence drew up and stars danced merrily – as if an encore to the main play. I stood entranced, watching one dazzling display of lights give way to another.

I must admit, I have a romantic heart. I wished my wife were here; that all my loved ones and friends were with me to share in this. For, romance is not the moments found in intimacy between partners alone, but a way of living in wonder, and with awe for the matchless creation that life really is. These were my thoughts as I pulled a writing pad from my pocket and a pen from its hiding place.

I struggled to jot down the feelings, blending the euphoria born from this spontaneous gift from above, with nostalgia for a time and a place I had never lived in. "How can that be?" I wondered as I furiously jotted down my impressions.

I thought of the waiter Jim, Miriam his date who called a happy greeting to me last night, and Miriam of Virginia, the young girl so enchanted with the *Hampton of Devon* story – the real reason I had come here in the first place. I couldn't help but see the "dots" – I simply did not know how they connected at this point.

I walked and penned my way past the bay and boat dock, not noticing my direction. I filled the pocket-size writing pad with these thoughts of peace, connectedness, and yet mystery; not unlike those I felt at the estate of the sickly owner where a noble and gentlemanly Sikh, known by name Harjot Singh, had entertained me for much of one day.

My physical hunger had been replaced by a taste common to me; the flavor of words that would flow from my heart to my pen, and as ink, remain a permanent record of who I was, where I was, what I was… I had quite lost myself to this until I found myself on the corner, above the quay, where I had started my bicycle journey this morning.

I gazed up the narrow ally-way which led to Singh's bike shop. A light shown in the store front window next door to it; from the pleasant antique book shop I had determined just this morning to visit soon. Now appeared to be that time, and much to my pleasant surprise, I found the store open.

"Hello…" I called, as I pushed the door open. I gazed around and found it completely silent inside. Making my way to the counter was difficult as I noticed shelves filled with books extinct from any ordinary book shop. These were rare, out of print, and apparently limited editions from the early 1900's and back. The volumes were not priced.

I wondered how anyone could leave this place so empty. It should be the busiest store in town. I was glad now that I had dismissed my urge to visit the more crowded night-life of High Street for my new addiction to sky-watching, which ultimately guided me here.

I glanced upon the title of one book standing alone by itself, face out toward me. My heart raced. My hands trembled as I reached for one of the "book of books" that had inspired me over a lifetime search for meaning and self-improvement. My mother first gave me a copy for my 19th birthday so many decades ago.*

I picked it up with reverence. I gingerly flipped open to the copyright page. "A first edition. Mint condition. Signed by the author!" I excitedly mumbled aloud. Forget food. Forget hotel bills. I would camp out for the next twenty days to save money to own this book!

"Hello!" I called to a clerk, who I was certain was simply unimpressed with my visit and somewhere in the back room. "Anybody home?" I called again, hitting the counter bell simultaneously. I searched in vain for a price. I did see an original sticker price but couldn't decipher the meaning of the British monetary sum of pounds and shillings first placed there in 1902.

I was torn between leaving it or taking it with a note, my name, where I could be reached, and offering to pay full asking price, whatever that may be. Finally, my reasoning caught up with my conscience and I placed the book on the counter with a note on the backside of a business card, explaining my desire to have this book, where I could be found, with a plea to, "…please sell it to no one else."

I placed the business card inside the front cover. I felt this respect, from an American author to a bookstore owner, might keep this edition, of a most inspiring original, safe for me alone to own.

I searched in vain for a telephone number but noted that the store hours were 9 AM to 5 PM. Next to Singh's, I determined I would be back first thing in the morning; be the first customer when I returned the bicycle to Singh's bike shop. I was miffed though as to how anyone could leave the store open after hours. All the lights on too. I looked at my watch. I had left the hotel at 5 PM and it was now 8 PM. I had consumed three hours!

"Impossible," I muttered as I left the literal, "Who's Who" of 19th and early 20th century English writers. As I closed the door behind me, it locked. I turned suddenly as the narrow side street went dark. The lights from the store had abruptly gone off with the street lights.

I scratched my head, mumbled some incoherent words of counsel to an overactive brain, and decided this might be the night I started to drink. After all, no one was watching, and this was home to the ale and brews where friendly pubs encouraged sociality. The George and Dragon, established circa 1390, was just a stone's throw away. Never having imbibed alcoholic beverages, the temptation was flirted with only momentarily. I needed sociality and my mind needed to slow down. I made my way for the city center instead and what I supposed would be an opportunity to collect my thoughts, get a good meal, try to let go of the excitement of finding such a rare and beloved book, and connect by cell phone with Jeanne, Mark; anybody to bring me back to my real world.

Once again I headed in the opposite direction of my intention. The bay was at my right as I strolled back along the landings and wharf of the small boat quay. There were men in skiffs and row boats, holding up hand lanterns as they fanned out, as if in search of something, or someone. I couldn't make out their appearance, although the night was star-filled with very faint tints and traces of the Aurora Borealis.

I forgot the idea of sneaking a beer at the George and Dragon, or a hot meal of English prime rib. I became engrossed in what I would later learn was a hunt for someone lost; but who it was, I could not know.

18

"A TIME TO EVERY PURPOSE..."

I made my way back to The Bath House Hotel in the familiar state of deep awareness for something observed. A bookstore such as this, those men in the skiffs not appearing dressed for our time, the inexplicable customs and ways of this remote coastal town of Devon... I felt I had been here a week, yet...

I arrived by train yesterday afternoon, didn't I? Or is this the end of the third day and I'm becoming so engrossed that it all has me literally losing track of time? I determined to check my last entry in the journal, and compare dates with the cell phone calendar which I used in place of a digital wristwatch.

I felt with so much happening in rapid succession – the unusual serendipitous happenings I like to refer to as "happy accidents" – that *time* had simply melted into one long week of travel starting in Lexington, Virginia.

Except for the unusual use of gas lit hand lanterns – the use of which was normal and common before battery hand held flashlights, or "torch" as the Brits like to say, the men in the skiffs appeared normal enough. *Perhaps just a drill of the local civil defense or something of the sort,* I reflected. My mind was upon these things, the rare book store, and that one book I knew I must have, as I turned the door key and entered my room.

I reached for the phone and called for room service to order "in." I was mentally exhausted and my explorations of High Street shops could wait another day. The restaurant answered and I asked for the "Special." Hanging up, my eyes caught hold of the hotel bill I had tossed on to the bed hours ago. I decided I might as well take a look at the "damages" for two days.

I opened the envelope but instead of a bill I found a concerned letter from the hotel management expressing their unease for my having been away from the room for two days without notifying them. Also it urged me to call home; that my wife had been trying to reach me and seemed extremely upset at not having heard from me. In fact they used the word "urgent."

Now my heart rate picked up a bit. This being out of touch for more than two days thing was some silly clerical nonsense, but Jeanne or one of the family could be hurt and "urgent" is not the kind of word I like to hear when traveling far from home. The hotel management also asked me to call them to receive a complimentary "courtesy call" home, at no additional long distance charges billed to my room.

"They really *must* be concerned to be willing to eat the charges" I mumbled. I dialed the front desk.

"Hello. Yes, this is Mr. Pratt in room 205." I said. "I'm calling regarding two things. I have a note here that states your records show I have been away for two days and that you would be accepting the charges for a long distance call to my home in the States?"

I listened.

"Yes that would be correct. I arrived on the evening of the 8th–

Last night, right?"

The sweet voiced young woman at the front desk paused. "Mr. Pratt. I do show you arriving in the late afternoon of the 8th. Sir, I must tell you that you seem confused. Tonight is the evening of the 10th. I show the only charges to your room, the meal of the 8th. This is correct, is it not?"

She was implying I lost one full day. I wasn't sure how to respond. "Can I have a few moments? I need to check some things. This is a bit confusing. I will call you right back."

My heart raced and perspiration formed on my brow as my breath corresponded to the experience of racing up a flight of stairs. I flipped the dial on the air conditioner to bring the room temperature down a bit. I walked over to a table where I had left my journal this morning. I opened it to look for the date and to see if my memory of what I had said was what I would find in ink. I read the final sentence to the entry. *Life is good. What matters more? Oct. 8th–*

I closed the journal, threw it onto the bed where I would package it in a FedEx envelope to Jeanne. I wanted her to keep it safe but to also show her I wasn't losing my mind.

My journal notes were about the night before, the fine meal, meeting Jim the waiter, the stunning sunset and Aurora Borealis, meeting another "Miriam" from afar, and about the unusually dressed patrons of the hotel restaurant – those dressed for a Victorian play or social. That was it.

I felt in my pocket for the coin Singh had given me. It was there, so today's experience was real. I picked up the phone, pulled a phone calling card from my wallet, and dialed Jeanne's cell phone. She answered.

Before I could say, *Hi honey, you okay?* Jeanne shouted across the Atlantic, "Jim! Where have you been! It's been three days! I was so worried! Don't ever do that again!"

"Hold the phone. Calm down! I called last night, and from London, early yesterday morning before I boarded the train for Barnstaple. I can never reach you with this silly special international cell phone thing I ordered off the Internet. I even got a message from Mark as if it were three days after he sent it. I've had nothing but problems with connecting since I got here. You didn't get my voice messages yet?"

"Yes. But you left London three days ago. You need to keep in touch more often than that! I get concerned, Jim."

"Hey. I don't want to upset you, but I have worried as much about you not calling back. And I didn't call from London three days ago. It was yesterday morning. I got here in the afternoon, and now I just finished my first full day of exploring. Anyway, is everything okay? You having a good time?"

"All okay. I was having a great time until my phone calls weren't returned."

"You called my cell phone?"

"Three times today and once each of the previous days."

"Hold on. You left four messages over two days?"

"Six messages over three days."

"Ugh… My head hurts."

"You took your high blood pressure meds? You have aspirin?"

"Yes. Not that kind of 'hurts'," I answered.

"What then?"

"Time. I'm confused. I seem to have lost it somewhere."

"Jim, are you okay? I mean where have you been?"

"I've been right here. I got here yesterday, had a nice meal, got proper rest, met some rather curious people, I'll admit. I went out for a bike ride this morning. Found a quaint Bed and Breakfast outside of town overlooking the ocean with this fellow from India. Old fashioned, but nice. And... This is what is strange; I came back this evening and lost one of the three days here. No big deal, *Right?*"

"Sweetheart?" Jeanne asked with a registered concern in her voice, implying possible early onset of Alzheimer's, "Would you do me a favor?"

"Yes," I cautiously replied.

"Come home. You've been through a lot during your flight from the States. It took you two days to get there. Then a full day just to unwind in London before traveling on to Ilfracombe. Then a half day of travel. Then you lose a day. It's understandable. Either you are extremely exhausted or you simply need to give up on this adventure before you do something..."

"Stupid?" I interjected.

"Not stupid. You just get carried away when you write, and you lose track of time and things, and what if something really does happen to you? You know. You get exhausted and confused and..."

"Woah! Slow down! I'm fine. Never felt better. This place is magical. I wish you were here. Something strange appears to be going on, I'll grant that, but there have been these Northern Lights this week. They may be interfering with communications is all. Atmospheric stuff. My Qwest cell phone at home gets messages sometimes a day and half after they are sent. I'm on the other side of the planet from you. But we aren't living in the days when mail or telegraph was the quickest form of communication. Just slow down and relax. I'm okay. Really."

"Really?" she asked.

"Honest. I'll tell you what. I'll call every day using this phone card. Could you do me a favor?"

"What?"

"Call Mark Kastleman and tell him to try me at this number." I then gave her the hotel's phone number with the international calling code. "You got it?" She read it back to me. "I'm having a great time. You just enjoy yourself and relax. Okay?"

"Just be safe."

"With your prayers I have always come home, haven't I?"

"Yes," she softly answered. "I love you," she added.

"I love you too, and can't wait to not only fill you in on all I am finding over here, but share this place with you. I want you to come here with me this time next year."

"Promise?"

"Absolutely. I'm going to find the author of *Hampton of Devon* if it kills me. Then I'm going to turn it into a bestseller. Then we are going to explore this countryside in search of its sequel."

"You are such a dreamer."

"But not boring," I said in self-defense.

She laughed. "No, life with you certainly is not dull."

"Just hang in their, baby. I will make you a rich writer's wife yet."

"Just not a rich widow, okay?"

We shared a final "I love you" before hanging up. Room service arrived. I tipped the server a couple of US $1's and asked, "You know Jim Hyde? He's a waiter in the restaurant."

"I'm sorry sir. No Jim Hyde that I know of."

"Well then. He must work another shift. Have a nice evening."

"The same to you, sir."

The hot plates on the service tray didn't stay filled long. I flipped on the television, caught up on the news with the BBC, and enjoyed some sort of chicken and dumpling along with a variety of greens, apple pie, and pudding.

Exhausted, I did the nightly routine of hot shower to clear the head and hit the sack refreshed. I pulled the journal open to write my day's adventures, but decided it could wait until morning. I was glad to hear from Jeanne and felt far more at ease. I looked forward to a call from Mark Kastleman, just to touch base with a friend and regular confidant. The "lost time" thing could wait until the morning. I was sure a mix up had occurred, and that it would all straighten itself out.

After a nightly devotion giving thanks to my Maker, I hit the light on the nightstand and pulled the covers back, eager to drift away into the rest this soft forgiving mattress and the down feather pillows would offer me.

It had been an unusual two days. A lot to ponder upon, and to read as given me by Harjot Singh. I was eager to get back to the book shop tomorrow and secure that copy of the 1st edition I had left there with a note and business card.

I wondered about the young couple, Jim and Miriam, and thought of Singh; the faraway-look he exhibited when I mentioned the boy's name. I would need to decide tomorrow if I was going to accept Harjot Singh's offer.

Perhaps he'll be at his bike shop in the morning. I'll just ask him to bring his friend's writings each day for use of the bike instead of room and board, I ruminated.

A good night's sleep always settles things and makes them a bit more clear by sunrise. I turned over on to my side and noticed my traveling companion on the nightstand. My little-boy conscience, and superstitious feelings of "bad luck" happening if I missed my routine, overcame the sleepy-headed me. I flipped the light back on and then let the Bible fall open. I read the first verse my eyes fell upon.

I have never been disappointed in ending my evening in this way. I smiled, satisfied that all was right in the world as the light went out once again. I rolled to face the window.

The fine lace curtain allowed light through and I thought I saw the last quivering movements of a celestial ballet as I lay there pondering upon the single verse I had just read from Ecclesiastes: *"A time to every purpose under Heaven,"* it said.

19
HEARTS OF THE FATHERS

I dream vividly all night, every night. I even dream during daily naps. I never feel quite rested as a result, but sleeping is never dull. In fact, I can usually glean some ideas for writing, or even have those sacred, but rare, night entertainments which inspire me, and lead me to accomplish something in my life I might not have otherwise considered.

But this morning I had to ask myself what was "real" from the last two days and what was not. I dreamt I was swimming home. That's right – from England across the Atlantic. I was in a boat with Singh, the waiter Jim Hyde and his sweetheart, Miriam. We were headed for Virginia when the boat stopped and Singh said, "You will be wanting to find your way…"

Then I suddenly found myself treading water as the small row boat headed back for shore, into the morning fog, and leaving me to decide whether I should try for America or try for the shore of Ilfracombe – a much closer and a smarter course. But I tried for home.

A strong wind came up and in my attempt to swim home I stayed in one place becoming more tired with each stroke of my arms to move me forward. I knew I was going to drown if I stayed here, and just when I was about to give up, my deceased father showed up. The wind stopped, and he said, "You're not done, son."

"Can you help me, Dad?" I asked as I treaded water.

"You must go back," he kindly voiced, seemingly unconcerned for me being in the water as he stood on a sidewalk.

"How far back?" I asked.

"All the way," he simply said.

"All the way to where?"

He turned to walk away but I could hear his thoughts, "You'll know."

"How?" I asked. But he was gone.

Then I awoke. He didn't answer me but I felt, as I awoke, a comfort within my heart that this was not one of those spicy food-induced dreams that I sometimes get along with a splitting headache upon awakening.

I had not intended to take Singh and his mystery friend, the owner of the country cottage, up on the electricity and modern convenience impaired Bed and Breakfast. I was sure Singh would simply allow me to have the pages, read them, and we'd just become friends. He'd be a great asset to me in this trip, I reasoned, but as for staying in a dream-land styled estate for a few weeks; it simply was not necessary – I did plenty of dreaming on my own.

This one though, with my Dad… These I pay attention to and so I felt I would at least need to read the pages Singh had given me last night and the note of explanation from the man he called "my Master."

"I'll read the pages from Singh's master in the morning," I sighed. I sat up in bed, scratched my head, looked for my bottle of water and an aspirin and then noticed the first beams of the early morning sun casting her rays upon the waters of the bay; clearly visible from my room's window facing west.

My water bottle sat on the nightstand with my favorite brand of headache calmer. Next to it, sat my traveling leather-bound conscience.

"Okay. One verse, to start a new day," I answered the nagging voice as I picked it up and let the Bible fall open. I read the first verse my eyes fell upon. It was the final verse of Malachi in the Old Testament.

> *"And he shall turn the heart of the fathers to the children, and the heart of the children to the fathers…"*

20
UNOPENED INVITATION

I couldn't quite shake the dream or the verse I had read this morning. I wanted to know what the "hearts of the fathers" had to do with me, this trip, and in general why it should be the last verse of the Old Testament.

I had put off reading the invitation letter Singh had given me. I was still uncomfortable with the idea of losing the spontaneity "hanging out" in a city gives; popping my head into a shop, the people you run into like Jim Hyde, even Singh; the things which provoke story ideas, and then there was my need to visit with the people in the book world who might help me on my way to discover who the *Hampton of Devon* author might be. After all, that was my purpose for being here in Ilfracombe.

I had eaten breakfast away from the Hotel. I found a café on High Street and was determined to spend as much time exploring around the town today as I could. I suppose it is my way of avoiding commitment. If I didn't open the invitation I wouldn't have to answer it. The longer I put it off, the longer I could linger in the serendipitous place of heart I enjoy being in – happy to discover new things seemingly by accident and seeing the mysterious hand of fate at work.

I wandered along the street observing people and window displays in an attitude of pure but simple enjoyment found in doing nothing specific. Having nothing to do but observe life is a good place to be in now and then. I get the sense that most of us are so busy with tasks, lists, and efficiency, that beauty – such as the Aurora Borealis had been during the several nights past – is often missed all together.

I noticed that now as people, seemingly in a hurry to get somewhere, did not acknowledge my smile or the "good day" I offered as they hurried by. I like to test the world out on smiles and offering a "how do you do" to strangers. Most often, I find people uncomfortable, but every now and then someone comes along, stops as if surprised, shyly smiles in return, and an exchange of good energy happens. Hard to explain, but the energy in a smile, or a well-meant "hello" is a blessing to me, so I figure it must be passed along.

That was my frame of mind as I finished walking the length of High Street in one direction and then ending up back at the hotel by late morning. A half-dozen or so Englishmen and women nodded, and two children waved back to me as I passed by, offering a wink and a hand waved "hello."

The weather was good, the sun shone, and I was happy to drink deeply of the moist salty air of the Atlantic wafting up from the bay along with the music of sea birds squawking for scraps of food along the beach.

I was going to go back into the hotel, retrieve the invitation from Singh, read it, get the duty of turning it down over with, but just then Mark called.

"Helloooo Markie!" I happily said, as I flipped the cell phone open.

"Top o' the mornin' to ya, Jimmy boy," he cheerily replied. "Thought I should see if you were ever going to answer my calls. Had me a bit worried."

"It's weird. I got your last message three days after you sent it… according to your message, but one day after I was in London, the day you said you sent it."

"Huh?"

"I know. It doesn't make sense. Anyway, your message and when you sent it is all too confusing to think about this early in the morning."

"What time is it over there?" Mark answered.

"Noon – Well, a little bit after noon."

"So you are keeping yourself the ever-early morning riser?" he teased.

"Aye lad. We Englishers are a people who don't always decide to follow the clock. Rather we allow the clock to follow us. Can't manage time, Mark my boy. You can only live in it."

"Hum… Well just checking to see if you were alive. Any adventures I should know about."

"Actually, since my last few in Virginia and New York I have experienced the quieter kind. Like slipping into another time and place. I'm seeing things I can't quite explain. I have to make a choice today about which road to adventure I will take."

"Sounds like… well, like… *you*. What are you thinking of getting yourself in to?" Mark kindly probed.

"There's this B&B outside of town. I'm thinking of working for my room and board. No modern conveniences, but peaceful."

"What?" Mark chuckled.

"The old man there – he's sick or something. I wandered across the place yesterday, or maybe the day before. I don't know. I seem to be losing track of time. Any way, he has this house manager. A fellow from India named Singh. He's a Sikh with a real dagger and everything. It's a real nice cottage out in the country over-looking the sea. And this turban wearing house manager fellow…"

"The guy from JFK?" Mark asked incredulously with a laugh.

"No, but maybe. I don't know. He hasn't said anything about 'going to the center.' Anyway, he invited me to stay if I'd read some manuscript pages the old guy will throw at me each day."

"Sooo… You are going to stay? Sounds kind of, well… spooky. What's the place like?"

"Old, but remodeled with Victorian furnishings. Remember the 1942 movie, *The Ghost and Mrs. Muir*?"

"Huh?"

"Never mind. It will be okay."

"What about the dagger-wearing Sikh?" Mark quizzed.

"Ah, that is nothing. My adventures back home were more dangerous. He's a pussy cat. Real decent man. Very proper."

"If you say so, Jim."

"I've got one problem though. I will be without electricity at this Bed and Breakfast and I am afraid I will not be able to call, unless I can escape on weekends to come into town for supplies. No electricity means no battery recharge for the cell phone either."

"You are going at this whole-hog. Real authentic," Mark laughed. "Aren't you a bit fearful? I mean it sounds like a set-up for a Stephen King novel more than a good James Michael Pratt historical romance."

"Maybe just what I need," I teased in reply.

"Hey, I have some information you might be interested in. About Ilfracombe," Mark added.

Then Mark proceeded to tell me about his and my favorite philosopher-author who once lived here, and that he thought I should check out what I might get from the locals in their libraries, museums, and bookstores.

"Funny you should say that. I found the strangest bookstore last night. I am headed back that way as we speak. It's filled with out-of-print books from the turn-of-the-century and back into the 1800's. In fact, our favorite book in question, a first edition, is sitting there with my name on it. I'm going there to see if I can afford it."

"If you can't, I can. Just see if there is an extra copy for me."

"You got it, Mark," I answered. I could see the street corner and side alley now which led to Singh's Bicycle Shop and the rare book store. "Hey, I'm almost there. I'll call you back later today. I have to decide if I am staying in the city or moving my stuff over to that Bed and Breakfast."

"Don't forget to call. I want one of those books," Mark finished. "And get his autograph, if you can!" he chuckled.

I thanked Mark for the friend that he is, and put the cell phone into my pocket as I walked up the ally toward the bike shop and bookstore. My heart picked up a beat as I neared. I was more than a bit surprised when I stood in front of Singh's to see… *Signs!*

"DANGER!" and "No Trespassing," and "Authorized Employees Only." Standing there in disbelief and mild shock I tried to sort out the illusion my mind was creating or the delusion my mind had experienced. I thought it a bad joke and turned to where the book store had been for an answer. Now I feared I was really losing it. The building where I picked up a bike and left my business card in a book was an empty lot with chain link fencing closing it off.

A woman, irritated that I was poking around near her town home in an obvious state of confusion, shouted, "Sir. What are you doing here?"

"I ah, well. I'm an American. Looking for ghosts actually."*

"What?"

"I, ah, was just wondering what happened," I answered with some hesitation. "The bike shop and book store…" I began.

"Book store? Bike shop? There hasn't been a book store for, oh, since before the war," the woman at least ten years my senior answered.

"The war? As in, World War Two? 1945?" I asked.

"Yes. That would be correct. A lot of businesses coming and going, but no book stores," she finished. The buildings were falling apart and then there was a fire. It was thought best to just take them down. There hasn't been a building on that lot since last year."

"Right…" I answered in barely audible tones. I turned, walked away, stopped once more to see the padlocked gate opening to an empty lot, and knew what I had to do. It was a long, slow walk, back to The Bath House, and an unopened invitation.

21

THE INVITATION

I found myself standing before the door of room 205, deep in thought. I was eager to call home; talk to my wife. It occurred to me that this entire trip from the start was a strange one; that I might be experiencing some sort of stress causing me to imagine things that were not real, or seeing real things but wrapped in too much imagination.

I paused, taking a seat upon the edge of the bed, and then fell back into it. I tried to sort out yesterday and then today's experience of finding two stores; Singh's and the rare book shop, now just an empty lot. I thought upon the name I saw on the counter. *The Bookery… Same name as the only book store in Lexington,* I silently posed. *Jeanne and Mark insisting I haven't returned calls over a three day period…* I mused. *I am losing it.*

I put my hands behind my head, brushing them against paper. I sat up and looked behind me to see the envelope containing the letter of invitation from the cottage owner on Lamp Hill.

"What the heck," I said, tearing the envelope open. I took from it an onion skin paper of transparent quality with elegant calligraphy styled handwriting. It began:

Mr. Pratt,

I hope you may feel comfortable being our guest for the time of your stay here in Ilfracombe. Though with a home in town, you have inquired as to my purposes in living here as well, and in not greeting you personally. I shall answer as best I am able.

I too have chosen to retreat from life and study the art of combining words with the intent of powerful delivery. I am not a wealthy man of means but have saved here and there to enjoy this privilege. I am now retired from the hum-drum existence of plotting accountants and big city conspiring merchants.

You may say I seek answers to the mysteries which plague so much of humanity, but especially how thought intersects with action. I have chosen this life, retired from the hectic worldly pace because of its appeal to me in seeking real truth. I begin my quest early each day upon these hills overlooking the Isle of Lundy and Welsh coast with a topic and then a simple interrogatory: "Why?" I then listen for the response, cultivated through the powers of quiet meditative silence along with the soothing sounds of the sea as my only companion. I then collect my thoughts in journals in hopes of formulating books for inspiration and self-improvement.

I do hope, Mr. Pratt, that you, a respected American novelist, shall find my humble musings worthy of your review. If this is acceptable, I shall deliver my daily handwritings to Singh who shall deliver them to you. Please forgive my aloofness. As a writer you understand it is not out of disrespect for others, but simple necessity for focus on the writing projects at hand while I nurse a lingering ill-

ness.

If you would simply respond to these ink blotter musings by addressing me with your reviews on a daily basis, I shall feel validated and continue to offer you additional pages.

You shall find in my cottage study, a writing desk with a roll top cover. I would be so honored for you to use it for your editing. In a slender drawer you shall find pages awaiting your reading each morning. Please mark them freely and then replace them. I shall send additional pages during each day of your stay.

Singh tells me you are looking for an eighteenth century love story and the author with origins in these parts of Devonshire. If that is so, perhaps by the end of your stay you may find what you are seeking.

I am sure you must wonder regarding my identity. I wish to remain anonymous for the purpose of making sure my writings are judged upon merit alone, and not local notoriety. When your thirty days are finished, you will know me. I do hope, Mr. Pratt, you accept my invitation."

Your servant at Lamp Hill Lane

"*Your servant at Lamp Hill Lane,*" I mumbled to myself. I reread the letter, then lay back in the bed and tried to not think too much. This offer, made at the precise hour of questioning my sanity, seemed to support my need to find a relaxing environment, get away from the city, not stay and find myself running into people like Jim the waiter who vanishes, and Singh's, "Now you see it, now you don't," bike shop and book store. "*By the way, where did Jim go?*" I muttered.

I wanted to ask him some questions about how he handled the other night on the bay, who the men in the search boats were, what he knew about the disappearing book store next to Singh's place... and Miriam. I'd like to meet her.

I sat up, looked around the room and decided to go out to visit with Singh and just follow my instinct. I felt around in my pocket for my room keys, wallet, and then realized I didn't have the "magical medallion" which Singh insisted I carry with me. I searched the dressers and my luggage, unable to locate it.

The night stand. I turned to see the only things sitting upon it were a bottle of aspirin and the bible. I remembered I had used the coin for a book marker. I opened to the page it marked. It was the verse I had read one night before; *A time to every purpose...*

I pocketed the coin and then called home. "Hi, it's just me," I said to the voice message. "I'll be staying out at a Bed and Breakfast for the weekend at Lamp Hill Lane. Not sure my cell phone will work. Not to worry. I'll leave contact information here at the hotel. I'm keeping my room open here so that I don't have to lug everything around. I'll explain more later. For now I leave you with this message:

"*In the land of fog and sea, where pleasant waters call to me, I play the bagpipes loud and clear, the mournful tune of yesteryear. I walk upon the quiet hill and yield my soul to silent will. And soon upon this sod I'll grow, another work you'll come to know.*"

"Love you, sweetheart. Having a good time. Call me and leave a message when you can."

I called Mark, got his voice-mail and left the same cryptic message. I like playing coded word-games with family and friends when I leave messages. Maybe it's the storyteller in me;

or the subdued wannabe entertainer. Not certain.

I just hoped Jeanne would not worry, and likewise I didn't want to leave my good buddy, Mark Kastleman, out of the information loop. I've gone missing for days before and then he'll call asking Jeanne if she's heard from me. Then the concern starts. So I try to leave comforting lines packed with a little "real Jim," the man she has come to know as a bit quirky, eccentric, but – hopefully – romantic.

I decided to send some things back home in a FedEx. I had kept my journal writing up until last night. I packaged it along with some photos I had developed of my stroll around Ilfracombe for the past several days. I had lost a journal in South America – one I had kept for years, and I didn't want to lose the words I had stored in this leather-bound diary. I scratched a note to Jeanne and placed it in the diary. It read:

"Should I end my life in search of truth, it will be a life well spent. As I reflect upon what matters most, it is legacy, a good name, and love left behind. Life is good. What matters more? I'll see you soon! Love, Jim."

I typed out a FedEx label on my laptop, printed it out from the traveling printer and slapped it on the package. I packed my clothes, the laptop with two charged batteries, and wandered down to the lobby leaving instructions with the front desk to charge my card for each day until I returned. I left them Jeanne's contact information and my cell phone number.

"Is every thing satisfactory, Mr. Pratt?" a concerned clerk inquired.

"Very," I answered. "I have been invited to stay as a guest for the weekend, possibly a week, at a residence on Lamp Hill just north of town."

"Lamp Hill?" he asked. "I haven't heard of any residence on a 'Lamp Hill,'" he added.

"Well, maybe you should get out more. A cottage on an old dirt road called Lamp Hill Lane above Torrs Walk. Quite nice."

"Very good then, sir. Have a nice stay and please let us know if we may be of any help."

"Actually you can be of some help. I'd like to Fed Ex this package home," I said as I handed it across the desk.

"Yes. We can take care of this for you. Will there be anything else?" he asked.

"You could help me by calling for a taxi," I answered.

"Right away sir." He quickly made the call and I gathered my things for the curb. I was determined to test the Bed and Breakfast situation out for the weekend and see what happened.

As I wandered out to the lobby to wait for the taxi, I pondered upon any meaning the verses from both last night and this morning: *"A time for every purpose under heaven…"* and *"…the hearts of the fathers."* I felt for the coin I had pocketed as the taxi arrived. I was now more eager than before to meet with Singh and ask him some rather pointed questions about Ilfracombe; the disappearing people, shops, and worth noting, my apparent losing track of a growing number of hours and days.

22
Lamp Hill

"Are you sure that is where you want to go?" the cabbie asked as I settled in. "The old Lamp Hill? I've only heard the hike path called that one other time."

"When?" I asked.

"From the hotel clerk who called me. Quite confused, I might add," he answered.

"Well. Let me help. Just up Torrs Walk. I'll point out the place. It's not used much."

"You aren't going to lug all that stuff along with you for a hike?"

"No sir. I'm staying a few days at the Bed and Breakfast; a private residence on the hill," I answered matter-of-fact like.

The cabbie raised his eyebrows then said, "Well, you are the customer," as he pulled away from the hotel.

I pulled the large envelope from my laptop bag, entirely forgetting that Singh had not only given me the "invitation" to ponder upon but also a few sheets of, "writings from my Master," as he put it.

It began with an intriguing introduction to a way to live with quiet resolve and serenity in a noisy world. I only had time for the first page as the driver slowed at the top of Torrs Walk and asked, "How far did you say, sir?"

"Just a bit more. When you see tall stands of trees where a lane with stone walls begins. There's a sign, clearly marked which reads, 'Not suitable for motor vehicles.'"

He shook his head and continued forward.

"There. Stop ahead."

"Are you certain, sir? There is nothing out here," he said.

"I was just here yesterday. Thank you very much," I said, handing him the required cab fare and a tip.

I looked back as he pulled away and could read his lips, "The man is completely daft."

So much for confirming my state of mind by coming out here, I thought. I picked up my small tote bag in one hand and my computer bag in the other and started up the lane bordered by the brush overgrown stone walls.

Once again I began to feel strangely at ease, carefree, and soothed by both the quiet of these hills and the distant rumble of the sea. A kettle-drum series of waves, crashing upon the bluffs ahead, echoed, and grew in volume as I drew closer. The only other noise invading my senses blended the ocean's with a rustling of autumn leaves upon the trees on either side of my walk up Lamp Hill Lane.

I stopped. I listened more carefully. So accustomed to human elements of constant communication and the travel type, I had failed to notice creatures of the wing singing in a carefree symphony. This was their world, and I now entered a parallel universe to our frenetic fancies and problematic pursuits.

Ilfracombe was as pleasant and unhurried as a town could be. Yet, there was something even more so about this cottage on a hill. It was as if removed from the world entirely. I reasoned that a parallel world would suit me well for one week; add to a state of relaxed well-being.

I reached the iron gate and passed around with my hand clinging to the entry token – a copper coin inscribed with this, among other messages; "Ex Tempore."

ACT III

EX TEMPORE

"In Consequence of Time"

23
The Victorian

I continued my walk up the now well-manicured but wheel-rutted lane. I expected to see Singh and the carriage any minute. I walked further and could now see the cottage roof line upon the other side of the hill's crest. "No Singh," I muttered. I again felt for the coin in my pocket, recalling his words from yesterday:

Please take care with the medallion, Mr. Pratt. It is the last of its kind and is a link to a purpose my master will be explaining. Have a very good evening. I look forward to our visit tomorrow."

I wondered what this was really all about. The carriage, the coin, and the quaint cottage so disconnected from the reality of life down the hill in Ilfracombe.

A smile crossed my face as a mental image, long ago hidden from memory, came to me. It was September 1966. I had been challenged by two Junior High School friends to sneak up the hill above the rail road tracks off Oak Lane and check out "this haunted house," as Bobby Boyle called it.

"No way! I'm not going to trespass on private property and get in trouble." But secretly the idea of checking out the ancient Victorian, a typical turn-of-the-century run-down farm home, intrigued me. We had lived in one when I was a small boy and imagining ghosts and their haunting of the halls was something of an adventure then.

"Are you chicken, Pratt? Bawk, bawk, bawk..." Bobby started.

"Weird stuff goes on up there. I've seen lights at night," I pointed out. "Besides, we could get caught," I insisted.

"Come on. No one will know. Pratt – you sissy!"

Not wanting to be teased anymore, I consented and up the backside of the hill we went. A half-hour of exploring empty rooms, old boxes stuffed with yellowed newspapers, private papers, and empty bottles, made it clear to us that the vacant house was obviously a hangout for kids wanting to sneak a smoke or a beer behind their parent's back.

The short story is, the house burned down two weeks later, the police came to my house, I told the foregoing story, and was confronted by a scary old woman threatening me with Juvenile Hall if I lied. I promised I hadn't touched anything and that it was a challenge by a friend.

"We'll be watching you," the nice officer said, and that was that. I never did find out how the house burned down, and I never explored abandoned or vacant Victorian style haunts of the kind again.*

At the end of my visit to 1966 I found myself standing before the pleasant cottage on the hill. I had entered the circular drive now and looked out to what I supposed was a carriage house. Instead of going directly to the front door and knocking, I decided to take a peek inside the barn-style carriage house and see if I could find Singh readying the buggy. I pulled at the left side of the large stable door and peered inside. I observed a well-maintained stable for the horse and provisions, but no horse and no carriage. I determined to walk around the back of the house and see if it had been parked near the garden area. No carriage and no Singh.

I returned to the front of the home and knocked upon the door. "Hello," I called. I turned the door knob, entered, and called again. "Hello? Singh? I've got my medallion. You here?" I ventured further inside and noticed upon the dining table, just adjacent to the kitchen, a handwritten note addressed to: "Master James Pratt."

"Dear James,

Thank you for accepting my invitation. I do hope you find your stay comfortable and relaxing. I have been required by my doctor to go to our home in town where I might be nearer to him and make it easier for my wife who attends to me in my illness. I have asked Singh to come early each day, bring the manuscript pages and make sure you have fresh victuals for your meals as we have no refrigeration nor electricity on Lamp Hill. I hope you do not mind that I offer these first pages for your daily readings.

In an attempt to become a better man I have amassed a sizeable library. Please enjoy the volumes at your leisure. May you find our Lamp Hill retreat as refreshing to mind and heart as I have. Please enjoy the home, though it be modest and simple.

—Your servant and fellow writer.

"Your servant and fellow writer. No name…" I whispered. I wandered out of doors. I was determined to know the grounds where I would spend this self-imposed isolation, for at least one weekend. The fenced back yard was in order. Bushes and foliage trimmed, flowers blooming, and the lawn well kept, I found myself at the gate leading to the neatly hoed rows of late summer vegetables. I wandered among them and pulled some peas from the vine. Breaking the pods open I enjoyed a handful of their fresh crisp flavor. As I reached the end of a row, I found myself before a tool shed.

I poked my head inside and noticed the finely kept and sharpened garden tools, clippers, snips, spades, and rakes, all stacked neatly beside a work bench.

Something upon the bench caught my eye. An afternoon shaft of light penetrated through the south facing window. A square object reflected the gleam from the sun. I walked over to it and found a glass-covered photograph placed in a newly constructed frame of oak. It was an obviously aged photo from the dress and appearance of the woman, and girl. I turned it over and noticed a handwritten note. "The owner's writing," I muttered.

"Taken this happy day of god-daughter's return from college."

"August, 1911. Nearly one hundred years ago. Strange," I mumbled, as I carefully placed the photo back on the work bench. "The man must be taking old handed-down family albums and framing ancestor's photos. Good idea."

I walked back into the sunlight and followed the afternoon blaze to the hilltop beyond the garden. There, through another gate and onto a grassy knoll, I found myself plopping to the ground to enjoy the view of a vast Atlantic Ocean. A couple miles away I noted the sleepy village of Lee. Sheep grazed in meadows as serenity blessed this land so far from the hustle and bustle of modern demands.

This place hasn't changed since that photo was taken, I thought. *Time seems so unimportant, so irrelevant here,* I mused, laying back into the carpet of green grass.

Taking in a deep breath of fresh sea air I thought I could happily live in a place like this, enjoying many years enhanced through the restorative energy as seemed to fill me now.

I instinctively propped my head upon my hands, closed my eyes, and allowed nothing to enter my mind but those thoughts which might spontaneously come. I started thinking about the days before. The encounter with Miriam, the walk and talk with her up to Washington & Lee University in Lexington, and the pleasantness which I felt in her presence; all flooded back into my mind now. Her innocence was real, and I felt I was breathing child-like life deeply into one tired of sophistry; the constant din of adult demands found in today's noisy world.

Perhaps because I was here now, in this quiet place, that feeling I had of being in her presence suddenly came to mind. Perhaps the photo I just gazed at triggered the image of my new friend Miriam from Lexington. *Perhaps…*

"Lee!" I said, sitting up and looking down the coast to the village beyond. "Lee Chapel!" I added, trying to sort through the spontaneity that mental awareness of dots connecting sometimes brings.

And then there was the Miriam I had yet to meet; Jim Hyde's girlfriend. So many coincidences had lined up in my life over the past week that I felt certain my *Hampton of Devon* author too, would soon appear.

I allowed my mind to wander more, and came to the story of *Hampton of Devon.* In it, on a coastal hillside, overlooking the harbor of Ilfracombe, Ensign Hampton Rhodes had last seen his Miriam.

I opened my eyes and noted that this spot, beyond a garden gate, but with the exception of the cottage in place of Lord Cavandish's mansion, was exactly as I had pictured the hillside where both Hampton Allen Rhodes and Miriam Cavandish enjoyed their last kiss. The romantic in me treasured the youthful energy of two who knew they were bound to go about a love affair with honor. "Magical," I whispered.

I felt I could easily enjoy a reinvigorating snooze in the sun this afternoon, but had the need to square away the guest room, read from the writings of the mysterious owner. I also wanted to check out the food stock. If I was cooking for myself for a few days I'd need to figure this out. The old guy didn't have a fridge, and I wondered about the water supply; both for bathing and drinking.

Picking myself up, I wandered back to the house. With no electricity, I decided to start figuring out how this house could be lit up at night, along with the other problems of survival without a microwave, outlets for my laptop, and charging for my cell phone. I was glad I had packed a half dozen bottled waters. Some conveniences a man should not have to do without. *Wonder if the bathrooms have…*

"Oh, don't tell me!" I blurted out as I came face to face with the small single-door structure situated twenty or so feet from the back of the cottage. Realizing I was alone, far from a flushing toilet, hot running water, and probably antibacterial soap, I decided one night total should do it here in paradise…

"Time to figure out how to light the lamps, now, before night settles in," I mumbled as I focused on preparations for hunkering down for a long night on this hill. I just hoped I didn't cause a fire tonight, the kind that had finished off the last haunted Victorian I had ventured to visit so many years ago.

Finishing cautionary preparations required for staying overnight, I next worked on a mid-afternoon meal of sandwiches made of a smoked ham and a homemade bread loaf which, I assumed, Singh had placed upon the counter for me. "No *'Grey Poupon,'*" I noticed. "What does this man put on his bread?" I asked as I chopped at a head of lettuce taken straight from the garden. "Plenty of jams," I noted as I picked up several bottles. *Must be for their crackers or crumpet goodies at tea time,* I decided while I hungrily attacked the sandwich.

"I got to get some mustard and mayo if I'm staying here long. Tonight, back in town," I determined. I went to my carrying case, found a bottle of water, and used it to help me down the lifeless meal.

Accomplishing first things first, (a hungry boy doesn't focus on his studies well,) I set about to inspect the home. I had already seen my guest bedroom. It was up a short flight of stairs situated above the study. My near six foot frame needed adjusting, so I found myself bowing my head as I walked, so as not to skim it against the ceiling. Spartan, but clean and charming, I found oil in the lamps, but again no electricity. I laid my bags out, put the cloths away, placed my Bible on the night stand, and my computer on a small study table.

How do they get anything done? I posed in silence. My modern needs were challenged at every step I took on this property.

I found the master bedroom locked, as I suspected it should be. It too was off the study but on the same level and with a view of the back of the property; a glimmering blue ocean just beyond the garden and hill's crest.

The study immediately became my favorite room. Airy, the study walls were opened with ample windows facing south and east allowing sunshine to act as natural lighting to the room, but also as a form of heat. I was delighted to see the walls lined with books, all of which dated no later than 1911.

Who needs 'The Bookery?' I thought with childish excitement most adults reserve for rides at a theme park. I was amazed, just as I had been yesterday while flipping through pages from those autographed copies I had seen in the foyer. I cruised through hard cover books boasting the names of Elliot, Tennyson, Dickens, Jane Austen, Victor Hugo, Thackery, Collins, Alexander Dumas, and...

"Lewis Carroll!" I tenderly picked up an original copy of his, *The Adventures of Alice in Wonderland,* and let out a hearty laugh; for this seemed like a sign to me – that after all I had been through on this trip, I was on the right path.

And, of course, the poets along with playwrights, Shakespeare being the most preeminent, occupied their place upon the bookcase shelves. American writers Hawthorne, Twain, and a host of lesser known writers; these filled seven entire bookcases from floor to ceiling. *Maybe I'm dead. This is heaven,* I grinned as one, then two hours of examining the titles went by in what seemed to me to be minutes.

I finally took a seat and enjoyed the crisp pages of books which should be colored with age, and fragile to handle at best. *This man has an immaculate sense of duty to his library*, I considered.

I needed these many hours for it to dawn on me that my eyes had need of, not only adjusting to a new environment, but to an older one as well; and it was one with a different time, pace, and charm to it.

In short, the few hours already spent here had introduced me to slowing down. The slowing down caused me to relax and look at my environment with new eyes. This kind of thinking may seem to some that I have too much time on my hands – that perhaps I should go get a job – that I spend too much time thinking an awful lot about nothing. However, my world of story-making is one where I process what lay before me, in plain view. It is how I am able to invent characters with differing points of view.

I was now beginning to understand the simple life required by the thinker who lived here. *But not living in the modern world is so disconnected*, I mused. *I could do this for a week; maybe*, I decided. *Connectivity, 24/7. That's the way to get somewhere*, I thought.

Considering the modern marvels of an info-saturated world where travel, world-wide cell phone access, satellite mapping with GPS coordinates, instant web, I-Pods, I-Phones, E-Books, and literal encyclopedias of information floating through the air, my life was indeed connected at light speed.

After many hours of pleasant perusal of books first published over 100 years earlier, it was time to earn my pay. I moved from a well-cushioned armchair to sit myself at the roll top desk situated in the center of the study. *Just like home*, I mused with amazement as I rolled the cover back. *OH! MY… Gosh!* I breathed.

"My time machine," I whispered aloud. *Unless this is a daydream*, I thought. *The kind indistinguishable from reality*, I added. The brass plate with the initials, of whom I assumed was an old London manufacturer, stared back at me. Every drawer, the desktop itself, the file holders, the mail slots… *The manufacturer must have made several*, I assured my over-active mind.

My hands tenderly swept across the cleared desk top. *Here I coax the writer's muse*, I silently considered. "The same muse who had given that yet unknown English author my story, *Hampton of Devon*," I finished aloud.

I sat there for some time. I searched every mental file to try to connect what I was feeling with the reality of my surroundings. I sensed that the writer who had created *Hampton of Devon* was close. I just knew it, yet I had no logical explanation for it to be possible. My hands pushed against the panel which defined the outside of the stacked drawers left of the table top. It gave, slid, and opened to…

"HA!" I laughed aloud. "The panel!" I belted out with boyish enthusiasm. Not even Jeanne knew about this feature in my own desk back home. I often hid important papers there; copies of documents I didn't want to lose by chance or misfortune, including a poor memory. There was nothing in the slot, the size of which could easily hold a ream of printing paper.

My energy was now high, and I was ready to go to work. I would first keep my promise, and then, with the use of laptop batteries, do some original work here at my Ilfracombe work station.

I pulled the table top drawer open and found, as expected, my assignment. Pulling a red ink pen from my shirt pocket, I began to read. The handwriting was in familiar style of the old man who owned this place.

The penmanship was, as I had earlier noted, superb. Very careful, the inked words were stylized with an old calligraphy or ink blotter pen requiring considerable time to produce. It read:

Introduction to Teachings in Power Thinking

James, once again I welcome you to this retreat upon Lamp Hill. Singh has named it thus for a purpose and I expect you shall discover the reasoning during your stay here. Allow me to set the stage, as one might in a play – for we are players in an important mortal drama, you and I. James, you seek a story and to know who I am. I seek to know your mind and heart for messages of no small urgency dedicated to a modern world on the brink of ruin, and clearly living at a maddening pace. The premise, therefore, which I shall establish for my writings, and upon which I also ask you to meditate during your stay here, is simply this:

PREMISE and CHALLENGE: The world, James, is in dire need of a renewal. Interest in uniting the energy of right thoughts with right actions has become diluted with distractions of a thousand kinds.

Rarely do we see this generation take time to ponder upon the gentle arts, the beauty of God's creations, the magnificence of a human life as a being of infinite worth and intelligence. We are lost to a thousand noises, interruptions, exigencies, fast foods, and fast moving of body and soul, giving little thought to the final destination of life. It is in the nature of the information and stimulus striving brain to accept distractions easily. Distractions force the mind to put off matters of serious import for those of lesser value. This is cerebral living at its worst, though the inventions for relaying and enjoying information is at humankind's highest level.

For six thousand years mankind has understood that the human heart was designed by an all wise Creator to be the soul's counselor and judge between right information and wrong. As right thoughts sow seeds of blessedness and joy, so those sowing destructive seeds of character and sorrow are mixed together in ways mankind's history has never before witnessed. Only a wise heart may discern and protect a vulnerable human soul from poor choices, in this information age.

The world, in a word my friend, worships information, addictions to pleasures too numerous to count, and speed of movement for body and soul over the best directions for movement of the same. Our world has become a fast-paced monster of demands straining individual physical and spiritual capacities, and breaking relationships which could achieve harmony and love. Technology has multiplied to the point it offers information in seconds; information of all kinds, good, bad, useful, useless.

My fear is that unless the inhabitants of our planet begin to use the speed of communicating ideas to slow down and enjoy the benefits of the same, the world will sow seeds of self-destruction from its own creations – information based wonders offering instantaneous fed gratifications and a sense of entitlement to constant pleasure. The brain will adapt and pursue more addictive qualities of pleasure to the point that the heart, our great inner guide, may break from over-stress. Thus in the brain's anxiety to have more, it kills its best friend, the life supplying heart.

THE IMPERATIVE: *My writings address this imperative for mankind: The brain must become ruled by the heart, a second more intuitive and gentler mind, where timeless truth is recognized, stored, and internalized.*

Why? Because the heart— the mighty counselor of the human soul— comes with a Divine mandate from God: To offer guidance that helps achieve His purpose for his creations: JOY. Subordinating the heart to the brain is neither a romantic way to live nor practical one. The heart creates life. It beats in the womb of the mother before the mighty brain is formed. It beats after mental consciousness dims. Indeed, the human heart is the soul's last light to go, and the concluding player on the stage of life before the mortal curtain falls and "Finis" ends the drama.

True it is that "thoughts become things" and are the precursor to all action, good or evil. Thoughts are things as surely as a blueprint is the foundation for the building which shall ultimately stand as witness to its pre-creation. Those thoughts most contemplated upon become internalized by the heart of man, and in turn acted upon with habitual regularity. Therefore, it was said anciently, "As a man thinketh, in his heart so shall he become." Let the heart counsel with the conscious mind of man and he will become as joy-filled as the powerful Creator intended. Let the brain alone guide him and like the many mirages upon the mighty Sahara, he will be drawn here and there, stumbling, grasping for visions of that which cannot satisfy nor save.

THE CALL: *James, my calling and yours is to deliver to readers a form of word-driven energy which offers a clear understanding of what will aid one in a quest to become a more powerful thinker, and thus have this joy of which I speak.*

Artists, poets, writers, musicians, all process thoughts with clarity others may deem abstract. They see, sense, feel, and hear long before ink is put to paper. It is the writer's duty and the artist's call, therefore, to translate their view of a thing into what others may come to enjoy whether it be upon canvas, the written page, or in a musical score which delights the heart and soul. The resulting combination of brain-born thought and heart-immersed intelligence is beauty and inspiration. This melodious harmony of energies brings the outward actions of a man in congruent cooperation with the inner spirit of the man.

THE PROCESS: *Knowing your divine and hereditary potential gives personal meaning. Establishing a purposeful life, then it follows that we identify talents and good desires. Our heart and mind alliance solidifies these through awareness and practice into a new meaning-filled history of joy and love.*

Before change comes, an inspired thought occurs. Inspired thinking gives birth to hope. But for change to be real and permanent, hope must continue to take form. As 'thoughts are things' we generally suppose thoughts must be brain-originated alone. This may be so for humankind who wishes to tap into the most rudimentary benefits of the magnificent mind. However, the man or woman seeking optimum thought power comes to understand that when thought from the thinking mind is internalized in the gentle heart, POWER THINKING is obtained. Thus "feelings," or "instincts," or "intuition," or perhaps what we have come to call the "sixth sense," comes into an alliance with calculated thinking to create dynamic and positive change.

Nothing could be needed more in a cerebral-centered world, so focused on acquiring more information at faster rates, than learning more power is available through slowing down enough to build a new awareness of personal meaning, then applying the heart and mind together to direct the soul's fondest dreams.

OUR MISSION: I wish you to accept my offer as a mission. You would not be here in this small village if you were not a highly mission-oriented soul. The mission is "our" message and is called, Power Thinking.

For this message to become palatable to a worldwide audience connected to their useful efficiency gadgets and electronic message-making I will require a ready mind, and a willing heart of a writer with influence. When I heard such a writer had come to visit our small village I thought that perhaps we could experiment upon this topic together.

I have chosen to expose you, James, my esteemed American colleague of the writing arts, to a philosophy as true as it is power-filled to change lives. And perhaps that is why you are in Ilfracombe? Perhaps our search for the same things has made this collaboration come to be?

PREPARATION: I choose then, to begin the topic of Power Thinking with examining life's Meaning and Purpose. But before I do I shall ask you to do something for me. I call it, "going fishing."

Take the rest of the day off. Work in the garden. Cook some wholesome foods. Breathe deeply of the fresh salty Atlantic air. Enjoy a good book by fire-light. Rest and allow your mind to travel paths it is not forced to. Ponder and think from the peace found here upon my hillside hide-a-way. Prepare your mind and heart. Put all other things aside for today except heart-centered thought. Do not strive to merely absorb more information. I shall look forward to your notes on the morrow when Singh retrieves these pages and delivers you more teachings. Sleep well my friend and enjoy the results from "going fishing."

-Your servant and fellow writer...

I looked up to the sunlight from the onion skin paper; several pages of them, which my eyes had been glued to and heart absorbed in. The cursive was immaculate, extremely unusual, not hurried or filled with errors as in our day of non-existent penmanship. I quickly did a 360 degree search of the office for a typewriter.

"One old-fashioned fellow," I muttered, as I examined my own handwritten notes scribbled upon my writing pad. The man had inspired something in me that rang of another time, another writer, and a bestselling book that had moved me toward these shores and my writing career three decades ago.

I quickly penned a note in red ink, and tried to make it legible. I have been accused of MD prescription style hand-writing techniques by my editors in New York, and even I could rarely make out what I scribble by hand. Slowly I penned:

"Sir. I congratulate you on the excellent premise for your 'Teachings on Powerful Thinking.' I find nothing to add but my *admiration at your careful penmanship and thorough study of the matter. I shall take your advice and spend the remainder of the day "fishing." I add my sincere appreciation at your hospitality, and I do hope we may meet one another. Perhaps there is a purpose, as you alluded, to our collaboration. I will endeavor to be worthy of your trust. May you soon be blessed with a complete restoration of health."*

A fellow writer and friend — James Pratt

I placed the papers back in the center drawer. Rising, I stretched, yawned, and wondered what to do next. I could obey the counsel of this wise new friend with no name. I thought about going to town and picking up the rest of my things and staying here for the entire week, but decided to put it off until after tomorrow's readings.

For now, I determined, I should experiment with the teacher's advice… and "go fishing." I looked out to the garden, picked myself up and headed to follow the owner's obvious technique for serving both his hunger and his mind.

I soon found myself examining rows of carrot tops and turnip greens, as I weeded around them. I instinctively did what I had seen my own father do in our backyard gardens many times. I picked a turnip and brushing off the dirt bit directly into it. As I did I could hear his voice, "Umm… Nothing like a fresh onion. We used to buy fresh onions from Arabs in North Africa during the War. When you are hungry nothing beats it, dirt and all!"

I looked around for some onions. It didn't take long to find the baby variety. Since I didn't have to impress anyone this day or night, I brushed the dirt from the small delectable and bit into it.

"Wow!" I voiced aloud. The sweetness, combined with the stinging in my eyes from onion juice which had inadvertently found its way to them with my first bite, surprised me. I looked for a water hose or faucet and not finding one, spied a well standing off near an aged oak just the other side of the tool shed. I carefully made my way there and worked the rope, pulling up a bucket filled with fresh spring water. I washed my eyes, but also tasted the water as I cupped my hands with it.

Delicious, I found a nearby cup and scooped it full with the cool, deep aquifer-fed well water. I looked for a place to sit and enjoy the moment and recover from the onion juice. I pulled up a seat on the ground against the several hundred year old oak which shaded the well and the nearby gardener's shed. Leaning into the tree, I closed my eyes and did as the gardener-poet asked of me. I allowed myself to simply unwind. I did not hear an actual voice but could imagine a gentle one instructing, "*…drink and be filled.*"

I obeyed and listened intently to the nothingness that occupied this land. I felt muscles relax; muscles I had forgotten existed. My eyelids grew heavy, but with something different than exhaustion. It seemed to be the normal response to a feeling of perfect safety and well-being. *Could be the water*, I posed silently.

My thoughts next went to my mother, still alive and longing to stay with us for our sake but reaching out to touch the hand of my father who long ago left his side of the poster bed for another place.* Then I recalled the dream from last night. In it I saw my father and he was guiding me back to shore.

"Can you help me, Dad?" I remember asking as I treaded water.

"You must go back," he had voiced.

"How far back?" I asked.

"All the way," he simply said.

"All the way to where?"

He turned to walk away but I could hear his thoughts, "You'll know."

I don't know how long I had dozed off but the rustling of wind had caused the door of the tool shed to flap. I even thought I heard his voice, "Time to get up and go to work, son…"*

I slowly arose, went to the bucket, and drank another cup of the magic elixir from the well, as I continued to rub my eyes awake. I did feel refreshed and grateful for simply enjoying this peaceful setting without any hurry or agenda. I wondered, in this simple but serendipitous state of being, what I should do next.

My hunger for words had retreated from my head to my stomach and I decided some greens would do nicely. With sandwich possibilities in the kitchen, and in keeping with the suggestion of the mystery owner of this estate, I picked some lettuce, grabbed at a few carrots, took some turnips and baby onions, then headed into the house to fix dinner.

The pump faucet was a nice touch. Nothing easy here, I figured out how to prime the pump, get it going, and washed up the greens. I decided my salad could use some dressing but remembered no refrigeration meant no bottled blue cheese or creamy style Italian. Finding a bottle of something that looked like oil, I tasted it first, determined it was olive oil, and loaded up the greens still freshly washed in the wooden bowl.

Slicing some bread, and adding some thinly cut smoked ham I searched the cupboards for something to add to it. A round of some sort of white cheese sat on a shelf above. I figured if I didn't die from it, I'd probably get some lactobacillus benefit. I grated some on the sandwich and greens.

Would like some Grey Poupon and mayonnaise though. Maybe Singh will show up and I can ask him if he's hiding them somewhere.

I wandered out to the garden, and stopped to look for a place to eat *a la picnic* style. I looked over to the oak tree, then past the garden to the hill overlooking the ocean. The sun was setting and the glow from what I assumed was the return of the Northern Lights, which had entertained me for several nights previous, appeared to replace the azure colored sky with its shimmering prism-like qualities. I chose the grassy hilltop for my eating spot and was not disappointed.

"The play begins," I said, as I alternated with bites into the sandwich and the well-oiled salad. I thought of nothing, just looked west out to sea and allowed whatever thought might entertain me most to play out as the Aurora's curtain raised.

After a myriad of memories from childhood innocence to the stresses of adulthood passed before me on the mental stage, my mind settled down with the disappearance of the Aurora's pleasant northern dance.

I lay back into the grass and simply counted stars, not by ones and twos, but by thousands as a galaxy of shimmering lights spread before me in the millions. I recalled doing this as a kid on summer nights in our backyard on Christine Avenue, wondering where God put the wall; the end of space.

I felt this also was Hampton's and Miriam's realization in their search for belonging to each other. I knew that this spot was an ideal setting for what the author of their story described as their last evening together and final kiss – while over-looking the bay of Ilfracombe.

I glanced north to Ilfracombe and faint lights from the nearby city reminded me it was still there.

"*You must go back,*" I thought I heard my father's voice say.

"How far back, Dad?" I answered mentally to an otherwise ghost.

The whisper came along with another calming reassurance that the world was fair and right, and with the stars aligned I was where I should be this night. And his soft voice? It was simply this:

"You'll know."

25
SINGH

I had finally retired to the upstairs guest room and easily fell into a complete restful sleep; not the fitful kind I had experienced since leaving home. No, this was as if the "sandman" had dusted the small upper chamber abundantly before I could even reach for the nightly ritual of opening the Bible, and like a fortune cookie offers, find the pearl of wisdom meant just for that day.

My head hit the pillow and I was out. Interestingly, for me, I had no dreams. I awoke with the first rays of sunlight piercing the thick cottage windows situated against the south wall to create the most abundance of natural light both upon sunrise, at mid-day, and at sunset.

I wondered about the bathing facilities and recalled the "out house." There was a water basin apparently filled by Singh yesterday, with a towel, soap, and a pitcher of water.

"Real authentic," I muttered as I slipped sandals on and headed down stairs and out back. Accomplishing as nature intended, and after sponge bathing, I went back upstairs, shaved, and determined to go scrounge for breakfast. When I opened the door to go back down stairs and to the kitchen, I almost knocked a tray over sitting just outside the door upon a portable folding table. A note greeted me attached to the silver plate cover.

"I trust you have slept well, Master James,
and that this simple fare is both filling and satisfying.
Darjot Singh."

I uncovered the plate and found hardboiled eggs, toast, butter, jams, and a medley of sliced fruits. "Nice," I offered to no one present. I took the tray below and sat at the kitchen table waiting for Singh to appear. I eagerly downed the entire plate and went to the kitchen counter and sliced additional bread from the loaf used for sandwiches from the day before. Adding butter and jam, I took the treats outside and enjoyed the fresh morning air. A light rain had cleansed everything on this hill and the pleasant aroma of bathed plant life encouraged me, along with the general beauty of my surroundings.

"Master James Pratt?" I heard. I whipped around to find Singh had quietly slipped up behind me. "I hope you have enjoyed a satisfactory sleep and found breakfast to your liking. How may I be of added service to you today?"

"Singh. You are very thoughtful. And I must say, I am glad to see you!" I added enthusiastically.

He offered a courteous but faint Mona Lisa purse of the lips but did not reply.

"See, I was beginning to think you were just a figment of my imagination, a ghost or something," I put forth with a chuckle.

He simply nodded and smiled as before. He seemed to be waiting for something.

"Is everything okay with your master? I mean his health?" I prodded.

Singh nodded and said, "My Master is hopeful that his health will soon be restored. He also wishes me to again thank you for the exchange of editing for your stay here. This seems to affect him in a beneficial way. And for that I personally thank you as well."

"Well, the mystery writer and owner of this estate has an elegant style and I find it equally beneficial to be reading his words. I have really felt refreshed by being here. Sleep was good, breakfast perfect. I guess I should get to work on reading and then I thought I would go back into town, unless…" I paused.

"Unless?" Singh asked.

"Unless you brought some *Grey Poupon*, and mayo," I chuckled. Singh returned my interrogatory with a blank, non-comprehending stare. "Mustard. Condiments for sandwiches," I added.

"The smoked ham and bread is not to your liking?" he answered with seriousness. "I could perhaps bring another meat, perhaps… cheeses of another sort?"

"I am fine. Just something funny I thought you'd recognize from the old television commercial, but then…" I paused and finished with, "I am fine and quite satisfied with everything."

"As you wish. But I must warn you. There will be no going to the property boundaries today. I must take the carriage to town and offer my master a ride to the physician who is occupied at his office and cannot make a house call this day. Then there is the matter of my shop," he added.

"Singh!"

He seemed startled.

"Excuse me, Singh," I said more quietly. "Have you closed your bike shop? And what gives with the old book store next to your shop? The Bookery? I went there to buy a book from one of my favorite authors, an Englishman from these parts, and the next day I found both gone! An empty lot sitting where a day before buildings stood is very strange. What gives?"

"Please accept my apologies. I cannot explain at this time why the buildings were removed. Will you trust me?"

I sat there wanting to press Singh. I'd learned long ago the first one to speak in a negotiation loses. I've been a lousy negotiator all my life. "Okay. I'll trust you," I replied.

"For now I shall see to your autographed book. The owner of the shop is the wife of my Master. With the illness of her husband she has been required to sell almost all the stores assets, repair to London, and use the monies for all the medical remedies and resources in order to help my Master recover from a long and tiresome illness."

"And what of your bicycle shop?" I asked.

"I have been privileged to help her cause and divested my belongings and bicycles to help pay for my Master's care."

I was touched at this devoted friend's selflessness but still bothered by Singh avoiding an answer relating to the building disappearance. I knew now wasn't the time, but really wanted to understand the building demo thing happening practically overnight. Maybe the answer is English efficiency, but I had owned a construction company for years before becoming an accepted writer and knew it to be practically impossible to tear down and haul off so much building material in one week, let alone in one day. Still, I determined pressing for an answer would not help get what I wanted.

"So…" I began, "May I ask the cause of his illness?"

"Anxious mind and heart, and the associated weakness coming from energy expended upon writings has created a neuralgia of sorts along with heaviness of lungs which, I fear is leading to a pneumonia. This is at least what the physician has declared. Such pain and weakening only intensifies as the cycle continues without improvement. I fear my Master cares so deeply about his remaining messages and another piece of written work most recently finished but unedited, that he is driving himself to an early grave," Singh offered, and then released the only emotion I had seen in him; a heavy pent up amount of air from deep within ample lungs.

"So… perhaps I could ride with you today and get to know your Master personally?" I asked, sensing a moment of weakness that might allow me to break with an unspoken protocol.

"That will not be possible. But he is determined to greet you at an appropriate time."

"This week?"

Singh simply smiled and then arose. "I must be on my way. I wish you a very pleasant remainder of this day. I have taken the liberty to retrieve your notes to my Master's writings and have delivered new ones for today's readings. They will be found in the usual place."

"Well then… Good day to you too, Singh. I shall probably see you tomorrow."

"I am certain of it. Good day to you, Master James," he said with a bow.

I was taken back by the tone of voice in which he referred to me as "Master James." There was something so honored, so dignified and kind, that I was left speechless. I simply stood and nodded, watching him exit out of my presence.

26
THE QUESTION

It was time to begin my work on the readings of the "Master" who I held a strange kinship for, especially since Singh had addressed me as "Master James," not once, but twice. He did so in a way that left me with the impression that it was not the first time, and yet *it was* the first time for me.

"You think too much," one of my six brothers was fond of telling me. Of course, being polite I usually did not respond in kind, but when I did I would remind him, "You think too little." We would both laugh and maintain our positions, quite sure of ourselves.

I was not sure of myself now. I wondered if I needed a reality check and determined this would be the last day I would stay here for this week upon Lamp Hill. I needed to find the *Hampton of Devon* author, call Jeanne and my friend Mark, take a break from so much serenity, find Jim the waiter at the hotel, and generally get some questions answered. *I could always come back. As long as I have the magic coin with me,* I chuckled inwardly.

I entered the study, placed myself at the desk and opened the top drawer. There, as Singh had promised, was a stack of writing, but not a simple ten or twenty pages, but more than one hundred – at least at first glance.

"Good then," I said to no one listening. "This really should be interesting. I should be finished by lunch," I assured myself out loud. Attached to the handwritten manuscript was a note. It read:

To my friend James—

I do hope you have found yourself rested, and now having 'gone fishing' you are ready for the deeper matters of my heart. Your honest appraisal of my work shall be greatly appreciated. Be sure to ask any question of me upon your final reading. I look forward to your candid comments.

Your servant and writing colleague…

I smiled and pulled the red ink pen from my pocket and proceeded to read, ready to make notations and edit as I did. I soon found myself engaged in reading the familiar style, but from another time and place. It was of an innocent era, that same one I had enjoyed with *Hampton of Devon*, as I read from the pen of a graceful thinker.

His elegance of style and thought had occurred to me last night, but never to the degree as it struck me now. I was easily entering this writer's head, and felt I was on a journey, both of philosophy and culture, far removed from the present moment.

After four hours I was exhausted, but not tired. Exhaustion was from emotional work required to process all that was triggered deep within me from reading the material at hand. I now had more questions than answers as I digested the transcendent truths proposed upon these handwritten pages.

Ten Principles were examined in detail in what the man called "Power Thinking." I decided I could not risk losing these concepts. I could not simply make hand-written notations and give it back to Singh. I wanted to keep this information and find a way to use it somehow; of course with permission.

I went to the bedroom I occupied, grabbed my laptop computer and returned to the desk where time had stood still for the entire morning. Hunger vanished. I began to type and remained at it until late into the afternoon. My excitement for a purpose in coming here was heightened, and not diminished.

I still needed to find the author of *Hampton of Devon*, but also clearly felt this man might be related to someone who was quite the literary hero to Ilfracombe; someone dead almost one hundred years, and whose original 1902 edition I had found a few nights back in the mysterious vanishing bookstore.

If this relationship was as my hunch suggested, this mystery writer friend of mine would have all the answers for which I had traveled across the ocean. I was excited, exhausted, thrilled at my discovery, and now too wound up to do much other than "go fishing."

When I finally finished inputing his handwritten text into my laptop I wrote a simple exclamation on his manuscript along with two questions in red ink on title page. The exclamation was: **"Grade, A+!"** The questions were: **"Who are you? Do you know the identity of the author of a story titled _Hampton of Devon_?"**

I did one more thing that I thought would be fun and romantic and old-fashioned. I pulled a piece of paper from a writing supply drawer and ancient crafted envelope with it. I wrote a letter of thanks and love to Jeanne and then addressed it, put a note on top asking Singh if wouldn't kindly mail it for me back in town, and sat it upon the writings of his "Master." I offered a one pound coin for postage, certain the value of two US dollars would be sufficient. *People don't hand write letters anymore. A shame. Should be fun for Jeanne to get this,* I posed.

As I closed my laptop and returned it to my room, I began to feel that the questions were actually one. This man might be who I had been searching for, and having done my part, keeping my end of the bargain, it was now time for the mystery to be moved forward towards an end that was my purpose in coming to Ilfracombe in the first place.

I reached to empty my pockets finding only the medallion – my token and entry into this fabulous world of Sikhs, Victorian hosts, wisdom-filled handwritings, and serene living. I read the Latin inscriptions, then placed it upon the dresser top.

I couldn't know it, as I lay myself upon the bed for a late afternoon nap, but the mystery was simply beginning.

27
GATE KEEPERS

The knock upon the door startled me. *Had I slept away an entire afternoon?* I squinted to see light streaming through the eastern facing window above my bed. "It should be sunset," I mumbled as I rubbed at my eyes. I lifted myself up to peer out another window, one facing south where sunset or sunrise would be easily apparent.

"Master James," I heard. "Breakfast awaits." It was Singh. I heard his footsteps and could discern they headed down upon the stair treads as I approached the door.

I splashed water upon my face from the wash bowl seated upon the vanity counter and then opened the door. A covered tray greeted me. "Thank you, Singh," I called.

"You are most welcome, Master James," he replied from below. "I will be needing to go to visit *our* Master. May your final stay in Ilfracombe be most blessed," he replied as he rounded a corner and stood facing me at the bottom of the stairs.

Our Master, I posed silently. "I see you have the pages," I yawned, pointing to the manuscript I had edited yesterday, then added, "What day is it?"

He laughed. "My Master's writings exhausted you, did they not?"

"Well, I... Uh–"

"No needing to explain, Master James," he interjected. "I have learned to listen to my Master in smaller portions, thus allowing myself to ponder upon the depth of his words before I take in a deep well filled with them. No one should drink the entire well at once," he said with another chuckle.

"Singh! I have never heard or seen you laugh before," I replied. "You look good in a smile."

Singh quickly resumed his stoic demeanor of the days before. "These have been hard days, Master James – only brightened by your presence here," he said. "I offer you a very good day and must be going. Sadly our town has lost two if its brightest stars. My wife in Lee, and I..." Singh dropped his head at a loss of words and I felt the urge to console. "I fear for the depth of feeling it may provoke in my Master and his beloved Lily," he softly finished.

I mentally noted the first hint of identity I had received. Singh had slipped. He gave me the name of my host's wife – the lady who had owned the disappearing book store back in town. He also offered his place of residence; the tiny village of Lee, just beyond these hills to the south. "Lee," I whispered as pieces to a puzzle started to fit in my mind.

"Singh," I began. "I am so sorry to hear of a loss affecting so many. You must have been very close."

"Yes," he sadly, but simply rejoined.

"Will you stay long enough to have breakfast with me and entertain a few of my questions?"

"I have eaten, Master James, but I have some moments before needing to depart."

Tray in hand, I followed Singh out to the garden table where I began to eat eggs, ham, and buttered toast with jam. He sat patiently waiting for my first question.

"Boy – I didn't realize how hungry I was. This is very good jam by the way," I stated as I finished a cup of freshly squeezed juice. "Who makes this stuff?" I asked, holding up the unlabeled jar.

"My Master's wife. She insists on wholesomeness. A vegetarian, her recipes are well known. The berries are straight from the vine."*

"Hum… Well. Singh I need to know a few things. I will be going in to town to call my wife and retrieve my other computer battery at the hotel."

His demeanor was lacking expression. I wasn't sure if he understood this testing of him or not. "And so I was wondering if I could swing by and visit with the owner of this estate and talk over some of the principles I read yesterday. The ten principles are not only fascinating, but something I think I could form into a useful book. Very wise, and very appropriate for our day? Don't you think?"

"Yes, Master James. Very wise, and very appropriate for your day."

There we go, I thought. *Your day. A hint into this man's mind… It's like Singh lives on another planet. Like a hippie left over from the 1968 Beatle's "Sergeant Pepper's Lonely Heart's Club Band."*

"You know George Harrison? John Lennon? They traveled to India a lot. Died a few years back."

Singh's eyebrows frowned in pensive processing of the question. He simply shook his head but began, "Do you have your medallion, Master James?"

"I believe it is upstairs on the counter."

"You will be needing it, if you are to go to Ilfracombe."

"Why?" *Now we are getting somewhere*, I thought.

"As you may have noticed, I am a 'gatekeeper' of sorts. We gatekeepers require a token, a ticket, some identity if we are to allow passage into a special place, such as this."

"But you know me, Singh," I protested.

"But do you?" he answered.

"Do I what?"

"Know yourself?"

I allowed silence to foster an appropriate reply. Sometimes the best response is another question. "Will you explain?"

"We are all gatekeepers to a world uniquely ours. Some control the gate with tokens, others with a simple open door. The most profound gate is that which lies within each of us. When you understand the gatekeeper to that world, and employ it with care, a universe of new possibilities awaits.

"In that universe you decide what you will become, what you will do, and how you will move within a world traveling at hyper-speeds.

"My Master has taught you that we are *what* we think about, which means we control or surrender our lives; the gatekeeper within must decide what is allowed and thus where we may go in life. At the gate, at the center of our world, is where we become empowered to travel anywhere, and to *any time*," he finished.*

I was moved by this answer. I could tell he had more to say but abruptly stopped.

"Soooo… Until I know how to slow my life and direct if from… some… gatekeeper, within? Some center of my being, I will need things like tokens, identities, passes, tickets?"

"You will know," he simply replied. He stood. "It has been delightful to chat with you, Master James. You shall find a note of thanks from our Master and instructions for the remainder of your stay," he finished.

"But... I..."

Singh did not tarry, but simply bowed respectfully, then exited through the gate, at the barn side of the cottage. His reliable horse and carriage awaited.

I picked up my tray, left it on the kitchen counter and then hurried to the parlor window to make sure I wasn't imagining all this. I saw Singh command the horse and the carriage began its way down the winding lane, to where I supposed was the other home owned by my writer friend. "Or his own home... Lee," I mused. *I should go down into to Lee,* I posed silently. *A short walk. Perhaps...**

I didn't have my watch with me, and the cell phone didn't work so I didn't know the exact hour nor day. I was rapidly losing a sense of time. "I'll check my Windows Outlook calendar on the laptop," I muttered. Accomplishing breakfast and the interesting chat with Singh, I found his statements and replies to my probing only left me with more questions, not less. I ran up stairs.

I opened up my laptop and pushed the "ON" button. "Come on now," I urged. No green light, no energy, no power. I searched the bag for another battery but recalled I had left it charging at the hotel. The cell phone was equally dead. *I need to get in to town anyway. Check in with Jeanne,* I decided. I readied my belongings into one bag and decided to grab the notes, or whatever Singh had left in the drawer of his Master's desk, and then walk down into town.

I noticed a gleam coming from the direction of the window and vanity, and then realized the rays of the morning sun coming in to the room, but now to my back as I closed the door behind me. "The medallion," I spoke as I retraced my steps to the vanity counter. If the sun had not hit just right, I would have not been reminded of my "entrance token" through a gate into this world Singh had so carefully guarded for his ill mentor of "right thinking."

Descending the steps, I felt that the lost time of yesterday – sleeping through the entire night – was an anomaly, yet a pleasant one. It had been driven from drinking the entire well of words the writer in question had caused me to want enough to spend four hours straight transcribing them to a file I named, *"Power Think Wisdoms from Lamp Hill."* If I ever wondered what had happened here, or if all this was merely a fanciful illusion, now I had the words stored safely to share with Jeanne or anyone else. *

I went to the study, sat at the desk for a moment, and stroked my hand across the table top. "Oops," I voiced. I had in my hand a pen, and by nature had taken it out from behind my ear ready to use. Now a scratch existed where only a smooth desk top had been before. I blinked at the site, recalling my own desk top at home.

I tenderly brushed my hand across the scar I caused in the polished desk top. "Yeah, but mine has burn marks all over the bottom of the four legs," I said aloud, as if to convince myself that what I was thinking really couldn't be.

I doubled over, still seated in the chair, and a sigh of anxiety was released in a rush from my lungs replaced with the relief that I wasn't totally mentally lost. "No burn marks."

Yet, there was enough coincidence, strangeness, and enchantment mixed together in this hill-top world to think, like Lewis Carrol's Alice – who having fallen from her world into another – that I might soon hear the Queen of Spades yell, "Off with his head."

I wasn't sure if removal of mine in exchange for another wasn't such a bad idea. I came to Ilfracombe for reasons altogether different than those I was now deeply committed to. I considered that my very vivid imagination, and the fact of spending so much time alone in self-talk, was causing me to "lose it," as we say.

The notes from the owner of this estate were in an envelope in the drawer; dutifully placed there by Singh. I threw the large envelope into my laptop bag and headed for the door, hurrying out and down the Lamp Hill Lane and back into the "fast pace" of the placid village a couple of miles down the hill.

Turning one final time, just to satisfy my mind on a matter, the cottage only disappeared from my view as the crest of the hill obscured it, and then as I passed completely around the gate, it faded altogether.

"Seeing is believing," I happily said as I enjoyed the scenery and pleasant stroll down the hill, onto Torrs Walk. The seaside town was in full view now.

"Ilfracombe, Devon, England," I muttered. *Jeanne really has to see this place.*

28
BELIEVING IS SEEING

They had arrived the night before. Tired, and not at all relaxed after spending a night in his room, she called her traveling partners.

"The Ilfracombe town Chief Constable called and said he would be here within an hour. I need to tidy the room and get all the information ready. See you in the lobby, say at nine?" The voice on the other end agreed. "See you then," she answered, hanging up.

She sat on the edge of the bed, still in a state of shock. This was not how she wanted to get to know the country he had spoken of with such fondness. So far she had maintained composure, but she wasn't sure how much more of that there would be. *Where did he go? And why did he keep this room rented. It had to be an accident,* she thought. *Over two weeks. Why didn't he leave a message? And the laptop battery? Still in the charger.*

She had gone over the scenario again and again in her mind. She lay back into the soft mattress and reviewed everything she could think of; just one more time so that the local police would have the best possible clues to help aid them in their search.

One Week Before

"Mark," she cried. "I'm nervous. It's been over a week. This isn't like Jim."

"You know Jim. How he gets into a story. He's probably just playing phone tag. He was telling me how his cell phone was acting up," Mark said, trying to console.

"Mark – Jim is a worry-wart. He always calls. Every day, sometimes two times a day. I'm the one in the marriage that can forget about calling. I wish it were that simple."

"What can I do to help?"

"I'm going to England to look for him. I've called the local authorities there. They have entered his rented room at the hotel where he was staying. It hasn't been used for almost two weeks. The maid service has reported that no one has been back since the day he left for a trip into the countryside. They said he was staying at a Bed and Breakfast on a hill outside of town. The cabbie he used to drop him off at Torrs Walk is being contacted."

"Yeah. I got the same message from Jim about some Bed and Breakfast he was going to stay at. He added about some old books at a quaint bookstore in town, and then went into getting invited for the weekend to stay at this cottage over-looking the bay, by some dagger-wearing Sikh from Punjab, India was kind of weird, but then…"

"You don't have to say it. I don't want to act overly concerned but it is just a bit creepy. No calls. Jim leaves for the weekend, doesn't come back. I could use some support."

"Let's go, then! We'll follow the clues he left. I'll call LaDawn, get two tickets and meet you in London. We'll all go over there and give him a piece of our mind when we find him."

"Oh Mark...you mean it? I'd love that! Can I email you my schedule? I know this is last minute and expensive. Let me pay for it. I could put it on my card and..."

"Nope! It's covered," he said, cutting her off.

Jeanne argued some more and then Mark finally got her to relent. "Jim got me several high-paying speaking gigs. I did well. I'll call you back with our travel plans just as soon as I get that email and secure the tickets." Mark could sense her emotions were high, and that she was struggling for composure. "And Jeanne?"

"Yes?" she answered, voice unsteady.

"We'll find him. You pray, LaDawn and I'll pray, and it is all going to be okay! Jim will probably call before we even leave."

She thanked him and then did as he said – prayed, just as she had been doing all night and day, but this time for thanks that Jim had such a wonderful friend to be buddies with.

Two days later

"Did Jim tell you about all the wild things that happened to him on his way to England a few weeks ago?" Jeanne asked as the train rolled out of the Paddington Station in London.

"Funny. Typical Jim. Hard to know if he really experienced them as he described," Mark answered.

"He's a story teller," Jeanne added with a hint of a smile.

There was quiet for many miles as the trio enjoyed what they could of a trip strained by the mystery of a disappearing husband and friend, now gone three weeks.

"I can't believe I am doing this," Jeanne offered after almost an hour of silent staring out the window to green countryside, and pleasant towns passing by.

"Me neither," LaDawn replied. She pointed to Mark. "He can sleep through anything. Then he awakens and the world is too slow for him. He's immediately back in the saddle."

"Jim can't sleep. Says he dreams all night. He's always suffered from that. When he finally gets started the world has already left the station," she added in an attempt at humor. "Maybe he's just sleeping it all off," she mumbled.

"Sleeping it off?" LaDawn asked.

Mark suddenly rubbed his eyes and chimed in, as if awake the entire time. "Jim's a dreamer. The world is too busy to be bothered with dreamers. He gets lost just looking for the train that's leaving the station, let alone trying to catch it. Jim should have been born 100 years ago."

"He says that all the time, with one exception. He thinks he should have been in World War Two. He really relates to his Dad's generation."

Mark chuckled. "He once told me he was in line with the other men being born in 1920 and got out of line to get a drink."

LaDawn giggled. "How does he explain missing that train?"

Mark finished, "Jim said that when he got back in line the war was over and it was 1953. So he came anyway."

All were enjoying the good natured banter, and Mark along with his wife had hoped their presence, along with reminiscing upon her husband's quirks, could help maintain a light mood as they faced potentially dire possibilities.

"I think I'll go see if I can stir up something to eat. I'll be right back with some snacks."

Jeanne and LaDawn continued to chat and admire the scenery as the train rolled toward its final station at Barnstaple, twenty miles south of the coast and Ilfracombe.

"Uh hmmm," Mark interrupted, clearing his throat. "I thought you both should see this," he said laying the newspaper out on the dining table for both to see.

"Get a load of this," Mark continued as he read the headline. <u>American Author Missing In Devon</u>.

Jeanne's eyes welled with tears as Mark read of every speculation from terror kidnapping, to accidental drowning, and even suicide.

"I'm sorry," Jeanne finally allowed, rising and running to the Ladies room.

"Mark, look what you did!" LaDawn scolded.

"Well, I didn't mean to. She was going to read it or find out anyway, I just thought…"

"She needs love. Just let the authorities handle breaking the news!" LaDawn instructed.

Scolded, Mark nodded as they both waited for Jeanne's return.

She scooted past them and in to her seat by the window. As the train conductor announced "Barnstaple, final stop!" Jeanne broke the silence. "He's alive. He's okay. I keep telling my head to believe, but I already know right here," she said patting her heart. "Believing is seeing," she finished.

LaDawn nodded in agreement and put her arm around Jeanne.

Mark smiled.

29
THE BATH HOUSE

After a lazy walk back in to town from Lamp Hill, I arrived at the hotel. I admit to having been deep in thought, with little else catching my attention. The previous three and a half days had been magical but also a bit disconcerting. I couldn't shake the feeling of having been disconnected from so much of what I considered "normal." I decided once I got back to the room I'd call home and then go to a restaurant and get a lot of stuff I'd been craving for days. *That should bring me back to earth*, I inwardly muttered.

Coming in the back entrance, I didn't bother to go to the front desk, but noticed several police officers in a conference with every person manning the front desk, and a half dozen other hotel employees milling around. "Hmmm. Crimes in this town are hard to imagine. This is hardly Central Park," I thought.

I made my way up stairs, and past walls decorated with old photos that reminisced of a bygone era when The Bath House Hotel was called by name, The Runnacleave. *That reminds me*, I mused. *I'm going down to the restaurant. I need to ask young Jim Hyde some questions.*

Turning the key to room 205, I was in for a surprise. "Someone has been sleeping in my room," I said aloud as I set the bags down. "Someone has been sleeping in my bed," I added. I walked over to it and inspected the cloths lying upon an unmade bedspread.

The shower was running. "Guess they don't call it The Bath House for nothing," I mumbled, wondering if I had the wrong room.

I quickly determined to slowly back away instead – no matter the "…*someone sleeping in my bed*…"– before being caught, and worse, accused of something I didn't do.

I almost made it to the door when I heard my name screamed by someone I hadn't seen for over one week. Caught by surprise, I turned and finished *The Three Bears* nursery rhyme in a mild state of shock saying, *"And there she is!"*

She ran to me, bath towel barely hanging from her, threw her arms around me, kissed me, then took my face in her hands. Peering deeply into my eyes she asked the question every man who comes back from a trip, (or back to his hotel room) wants to hear: "Honey where have you been?"

"Well... I'll leave more often to get this kind of reception," I answered teasingly.

"Stop it!" she scolded, pulling me onto to the bed to sit next to her. "Where have you been all this time!"

"Sweetheart. I meant to call, I..."

"YOU MEANT TO CALL! What where you thinking!" she demanded loudly.

"I, ah well, see – it was the weekend... and, uh, well, the cell phone reception is bad. I was staying out at this bed and breakfast place see... called Lamp Hill Lane – just outside of town – and I figured I'd call when I got back here; at the hotel. What are you doing here?"

"Are you kidding?" she tried in softer tone. "You think I would go two weeks and hear nothing and not come looking?"

"Well, you know my trip is for three weeks. I've barely begun. It's been a week ago yesterday and..."

"ONE WEEK AGO YESTERDAY!" she shouted. Then calming herself, "Jim – it's going on three weeks as of yesterday!" she offered in more hushed tones. Tears were starting to brim in her eyes now.

There was a knock at the door. I was in a semi-aware state that this was real, and not a dream, and that Jeanne really was here. *Although,* I thought, *In a few of those she isn't wearing...*

"JIM!" she scolded, as she arose and grabbed the cloths laid out on the bed. "It's probably Mark and LaDawn. Answer the door! I'll be right out. AND YOU HAVE SOME EXPLAINING TO DO!" she snapped as the bathroom door closed behind her.

Another knock.

"I could be asleep; under the tree up at Lamp Hill," I considered. I thought about it and went to the bathroom door. My head hurt suddenly. I wake up often with headaches, but sleep through them. I figured I'd test this out. "Jeanne!" I called.

"ANSWER THE DOOR!" she called back.

Hummm... Curious... Three weeks and a day... right... I mumbled as the knocking grew louder.

"Hey Jimbo! That you?" he called.

It is either Mark Kastleman, or someone who sounds a lot like him, I spoke quietly in disbelieving self-talk. I opened the door, my mouth fell open, and there standing before me was...

"Naw!"

My mind swam for a reason to reassure myself that I was not transported to another realm... to a place of another dimension; to the...

"Hey brother!" he laughed. "Good to see you man!" he added as he bounced through the door. After a brotherly "abrazo" he stood back. "Hey Jim. You are okay! I thought…"

"I was dead," I said flatly. "Come in. I need someone to tell me what's going on."

He pulled up a chair, at the small table adjoining the bed, and by the picture window.

"I thought I heard Jeanne. She here?" he asked.

"In the bathroom," I answered, still not sure if this was real.

"Hey brother? You okay? Where you been?" Mark pursued.

"I've been okay. Here in town. Near by. Up at that cottage on the hill I told you about the other day"

"You mean that house you told me about before the cell phone went dead a couple weeks back?"

"Hold that thought," I said.

I reached into my pocket and turned the cell phone on. I watched for it to light up and the chime to sound. "You have twelve messages," a friendly voice said after I hit the "Voice Message" button. I listened to several worried voices; Jeanne, Mark, the hotel manager, a local police officer, my brother, my son, daughter, and she was actually crying.

"Mark – I'm a bit concerned. How long you guys been here looking for me?"

"We got in to London this morning and came straight here. Hey there's…"

"Hi LaDawn," I called out as she appeared at the open door.

"Jim where have you been!" she shouted.

"Actually, I'm not sure," I answered, now thoroughly used to the question.

LaDawn entered and suddenly both Mark and his wife fell into a respectful silence, noting my thoughts were deep and filled with processing some things that didn't connect to the same timeline dots as theirs.

I got up from the chair, and motioned for LaDawn to please come in and take my seat at the table. I then swung myself onto the bed, and with hands behind my head, closed my eyes to the sound of Jeanne's blow-dryer in the bathroom and Mark's question…

"Jim, do you need a doctor?"

"I feel fine. A headache is all. I just don't understand what's going on with the time thing. I feel like I have lost something, except…"

Silence…

"Except," Jeanne softly asked, now out from the bathroom.

"Except, I'm really glad you are here with me in Ilfracombe," I quietly offered. "I have some things to share, a place I want you to see. If what you are suggesting is true… If I really have been gone from home more than a week… If this isn't some kind of joke, then I'll need all the support I can get.

"See, I've either just come out of, or am entering a marvelous dream and don't want to 'adjust my TV set…'" I felt hot moisture suddenly sting my eyes. I tried to hide the emotions.

"Jim, honey," Jeanne sweetly voiced as she lay her head upon my shoulder. "I don't understand, but I love you and will help you."

I stared straight ahead, in a stunned semi-awareness that Singh might not be who he really was to me, nor the mysterious "Master" of Lamp Hill Lane. Respectful quiet greeted my reverie. All I could do was allow one whispered thought:

"You are about to enter… The Twilight Zone…"

32
"What Ifs"

The first thing I asked of Mark, LaDawn, and Jeanne was to call the police, let them know there was a mix-up and to please call off the "Network News" crews waiting in the hotel lobby for some word on my re-appearance.

We agreed it was best that I craft a carefully worded statement and that Mark be the one to take it to the cadre of news from the MSNBC, BBC, CBS, CNN, FOX, ABC, and other networks interested in the "disappearing American author" story.

Mark picked up the phone and called the hotel, then the police as I sat in silence with my thoughts, and I suppose Jeanne and LaDawn with theirs.

I was sure I couldn't leave the room with all the commotion downstairs. I needed to eat. I knew if we could sneak out to dinner, and then drive out to Lamp Hill, explaining the entire story as we went, that all would become settled. There would be some explanation for the missing time when push came to shove, and maybe I was a bit "off" – mentally, emotionally; whatever.

After all, more than one artsy person has been called "genius." A disservice by fans or admirers when referred to as such, in fact the creative artist mind is usually so burdened with the crafting of the work that they lose things; a lot of things. Time would be just one of the many things a creative person might misplace. Our kind of sanity is someone else's crazy. Everyone knew I didn't carry a calendar, day planner, care much for my Internet devices that kept track of appointments, and such.

So I'm not the most organized in some areas. It takes a heck of a lot of organization of another kind to create a novel or any other kind of published work, I consoled my mind.

After some minutes, Mark finished his calls. We began to discuss what to do with our time here in England. I knew what they were thinking: "Jim has finally lost it and needs to relax his mind. How can we best accomplish that?"

Mark started first. "I hear Devon is close to Camelot country. Jim's favorite movie and story; right Jim?"

"Yep," I answered quietly.

"We need to avoid the cameras and news people," Jeanne interjected.

"We probably should hire a driver for the entire day. Someone who knows Devon," LaDawn added. "You know, just in case we are found; and followed or something."

"I'd like that," I assured softly. "I need to think; just be with you guys."

"Done. I'll call the concierge," Mark stated.

He dialed, identified himself as a guest, but deftly done without using his name. A list of three tour companies was provided and Mark was quickly on the phone making plans with one that stood out.

"I want to show you guys where I've been," I voiced to Jeanne and LaDawn.

"Let's make our escape, grab a bite to eat somewhere out of Ilfracombe. I think that is best. Then tonight or something you can point the place out to us," my wife answered.

I was suspicious she was trying to spare my nervous brain from a breakdown, and so I simply nodded in approval.

"Thank you, Mr. Hyde," Mark finished.

"What! Who did you say?"

"The concierge?"

"Yes! The Concierge!" I demanded.

"Jim, hold on. What's so important about the name?" Mark asked.

Jeanne instinctively grabbed my arm.

"Did he give you his first name?"

"Yes. You and he share it. It's James."

"I've got to go see him. Right now!" I got up and headed to the door, but Mark four inches taller, blocked it and gently put his hand upon my shoulder.

"Jim, we are leaving through the back. The news camera crews are still down there. Mr. Hyde promised he would cover for us. The tour guide will be here in twenty minutes. Meeting Mr. Hyde can wait."

"Right," I simply stated. And Mark was right, of course. Mark is always right. He's the cooler head of the two of us. Less impulsive, more thoughtful and pragmatic, it is what makes him a great non-fiction writer and speaker. He has enthusiasm for nearly all the same things I do, but has managed to learn how to bridle that enthusiasm and channel it to its best end result.

I nodded, relaxed and then thought about the meaning of the word "concierge." I pulled out a pocket thesaurus from my computer bag and looked it up as everyone just silently looked on.

I smiled in satisfaction and simply stated aloud, *"Gatekeeper. It means gatekeeper. Now that makes perfect sense."*

Jeanne, LaDawn, and Mark had "no clue," but I was beginning to see them; clues of course, through the prism of the fiction novelist who often sees things in a way others may simply pass by without a second glance.

See, we get "glimpses" through asking the many "what ifs" and possibilities not yet written in book or script. Some pieces of a puzzle to my stay in Ilfracombe, now were beginning to fall into place. As for me, I would play my part – the lost soul – but quietly find the answers to the many, "what ifs."

FINALE

EX ANIMO

"Through the Heart"

33
RETURN TO INNOCENCE

I slipped out early. We had spent the afternoon into the late evening touring southern Devon and Cornwall. Mark arranged a tour of the Tintagel Castle, one of the probable sites of King Arthur's Camelot.

I knew the trio, who came to England to rescue me from my delusional mind, were trying their best to play as if it were all normal, the loss of time and such. They laughed, joked and gingerly side-stepped the enormity that was the incongruence between how many days I remember spending here and how many days everyone, including news media, believed I was missing.

I knew that my psychological state was fragile, and of course so did they. I allowed them to feed doses of reality in teaspoon measurements – amounts acceptable to bringing me out of wherever I had been in my mind – but my heart told me I was not delusional; that I had met people known only to me, and that they were *real*.

So now I was on my way to find out. Jeanne is a deep sleeper, and we all were exhausted. We agreed to a late start today; to just sleep in and take it easy. We would order breakfast in and slip out through the back stairs. There were still a few news reporters willing to tell the "rest of the story" about the missing American author. I just wanted to get to London and back home to the states.

But there were two things I must do. And I had to do them early. I had to find Jim Hyde – restaurant waiter, and presumably now hotel concierge who Mark had talked to, and I had to go to Lamp Hill Lane; *alone*.

The first one was easy. I left a note at the concierge's desk reminding "James Hyde" of his former "waiter" role at The Bath House Hotel, and that I would like to speak to him. I left him my cell phone number.

The second item of the early dawn was a bit more complicated. I needed to see for myself, by myself, if yesterday's visit with the Constable were all just an illusion. As I walked in the pre-dawn hours up Granville road and then Torrs Walk toward my destination, that part of our day, yesterday's midday escort by Chief Constable White to Lamp Hill Lane re-visited my mind:

Yesterday

There had been a last minute call to the room. Mark took it and then pulled Jeanne aside to explain.

"What?" I asked. "Come on. Give it to me," I insisted.

"Before leaving for the rest of the day," Jeanne began, "we need to clear something up.

I've asked Chief Constable White, who had been in charge of your 'Missing Persons' case, to take us to Lamp Hill Lane."

"To prove I'm crazy. You know, get it out of the way," I retorted with irritation.

Silence…

"Jim…" Mark replied. "A lot of people spent considerable time wondering where you were; even if you were alive. We owe them," he said.

I looked at Jeanne. She brought her eyes up to meet mine. I looked at everyone in the hotel room. "Okay. Let's get it over with."

"We're meeting him in the lobby first, then going up to Lamp Hill Lane," Jeanne added. "News people will be there waiting."

"I thought we were escaping the reporters. Sneak out of town. How are we going to pull that off now?"

"He insisted," Mark said. "Seems the Chief Constable needs good publicity after spending all the time over the last week."

"We feel this will settle it. Get everything out of the way so we can go enjoy the day," LaDawn cheerily added.

"Well… You three love me, even if I am crazy. And, I did put you all on the spot. Why not? I'll confess, take the heat. Let's go." I secretly was okay with this. Now I could spot Jim Hyde the concierge in the crowd, pull him aside, and get some questions answered.

Mark made a call, alerting the Front Desk to our coming out into the public eye, then we headed down to the lobby and were immediately confronted with flashing cameras, as Police Chief Constable White waved us to the front of the "Press Conference" podium, now located outside in the ample parking lot.

"Well then. We are glad to announce the safe return of Mr. James Pratt, American author," he began. "It makes us gratified to know his family and friends were so willing to do whatever it took to assure his safety. It is our understanding that Mr. Pratt and his wife were in touch after all; and as to the time lost between communications and calls, I will now allow Mr. Pratt a few words with the Press."

Constable White stepped back, and that was my cue to step forward. I cleared my throat. I gazed over the crowd. *No Jim Hyde,* I inwardly voiced in disappointment.

"Ah, this is somewhat awkward and embarrassing. I want to thank Ilfracombe's Police Chief White, his fine staff, The Bath House Hotel staff, and all those so concerned with my whereabouts and safety. I need to confess to you that I lost track of time and simply made judgment errors regarding the way I chose to keep in touch with home. For that I apologize to all, especially my long-suffering wife Jeanne, and friends Mark and LaDawn."

"Mr. Pratt," a female journalist called out. "Can you tell us precisely where you have been?"

"I could write a book about it," I answered simply.

"Sir. Have you any health problems contributing to your becoming missing? Some have suggested you located a small Bed and Breakfast and were ill for all these days. How is your health, if you don't mind me asking?"

"You mean my mental state? Well, I could write something on that, but it would be about my heart, and for now it seems to be ticking on schedule. I was at a Bed and Breakfast and in fact worked for my room and board there. All I can say is the owner and his Indian house manager; they are…"

"That will be all," Chief Constable White said, interrupting. "As you can see, Mr. Pratt is alive and well. I am sure he will release an official statement which we will be happy to make public. Thank you all," he finished. He then escorted our party, surrounded by local officers, to the cars waiting outside the hotel.

"That went well," I said.

"Let's clear out of Dodge," Mark offered, holding the cab door open for us. "I've asked Constable White to come along. LaDawn and I will follow in a rental car."

Jeanne entered the cab, I followed, with Chief Constable White up front with the cabbie. What followed is what caused me to leave the hotel early this morning, just to reassure myself that I could regain something now missing.

ॐ

"I hope you can see this from my perspective, sir. I really did enjoy several days on Lamp Hill," I said, as we drove up Torrs Walk.

"I have no doubt of that, Mr. Pratt," Chief Constable White said.

"You'll see," I whispered in Jeanne's ear.

She just nodded and squeezed my hand in reassurance.

"Here! Pull over here!" I looked back to see if Mark was following. He pulled behind the cab. "See! Look at that beat-up sign. Right there!" I said pointing. 'Not suitable for motor vehicles.' HA! Just like I told you!" I eagerly jumped out and pointed up the winding trail, overgrown with weeds. "This way," I eagerly announced with a wave of my hand as I forged ahead. I wanted to make sure it was there and was more worried about my sanity than anyone could know. I looked back once to see Jeanne, Chief Constable White, Mark and LaDawn trailing about twenty paces behind.

ॐ

"Mr. White," Jeanne quietly voiced. "Thank you for indulging Jim on his fantasy so we can help him get it out of his system."

"Mrs. Pratt," the Police Chief answered, "I can quite assure you that the property in question has not seen house nor home for quite some many years. However, I am most happy to escort you here and help in any fashion possible."

"I hope Jim doesn't fall apart," Mark whispered to LaDawn.

"Me too."

"Somehow things will finally click with Jim and he will return to normal," Mark reassured himself in quiet talk with his wife. "I've seen him this way before. He'll connect the dots."

"Hope so," Jeanne whispered, overhearing. "Look at him. Like an excited little boy," she added as they walked up the tree-lined drive.

ॐ

"Almost there," I yelled. "Come on. I'll show you where I've been. Singh will probably show up in the carriage," I nervously laughed. "It's just around this bend. See, there…" I said, with a sudden jolt stopping me from planting one more foot in front of the other. "Where did the iron gate go?" I whispered.

My heart picked up a beat as I noticed the weathered wooden fencing and gate now occupying the place of a private wrought iron one where I had previously met Singh. A small sign read, "Entering National Trust hiking area. Caution grazing animals."

The hill appeared nearly vacant. The road leading through the grassy hill up to the crest and beyond, still bore deep ruts from wheels as narrow as the carriage. This calmed me a bit.*

I forced myself to move forward and walked past the posts where the iron gate had been just yesterday. I examined the course rocky drive, full of grass now; not so carefully manicured with fine gravel as I was accustomed. I stopped, unaware of the presence of the others as my mind swam for answers. The winding lane led up some two hundred yards more to a peak, where the scenic coast and that of the cottage came into full view.

The others remained a respectful distance behind me, chatting, enjoying the breath taking vistas, and bucolic pastures dotted with grazing sheep. I was nervous but hopeful as we hiked on. Nothing could have prepared me for what my mind clearly told me was impossible but which my eyes told me was indeed, a fact.

"Been like this for some ninety years now, Mr. Pratt," the Chief Constable said, catching up to me. "Stone, brick, and rubble," he added.

The Police Chief sensed my confusion as Jeanne, Mark, and LaDawn came up along side me.

"Since the First World War," he continued. "A fire was lit. There was a coast watchman who rented the place on lookout for German submarines and such. One night, the tale goes, as the watchman left his post for town and supplies, the old home went ablaze. Some suspect arson. No one really knows. All that was left was a piece of furniture, a desk I believe, that miraculously survived with the owner's papers in it. But it has long since disappeared. That's the tale and legend of Lamp Hill. Not many people come here. A few picnicking sorts. Some think the land is *haunted*... But most of England is haunted," he said with a laugh. "Wizards, dead knights, fairies, men driving empty carriages, trolls, ghosts of lovers lost at sea..." he added. "The stuff of *make believe*," he emphasized.

I slowly turned, and looked at each of the members of the party. "Right," I simply replied.

"I believe you'd call it *fiction*," the police chief added.

"I get the point," I answered.

I decided to smile through it, though faking emotion is difficult for me. I felt my eyes sting. I missed Singh like one does an old friend. And the enchanted place, with the mystery writer, was a bit of heaven removed from this planet of tumult and noise; the likes I had rarely known on my travels far and wide. "*A privileged place*," I muttered.

"Jim? Honey? You okay," Jeanne asked as she came up beside me.

I reached for her hand and shook my head. "Well," I announced. "I just... uh, wanted to... uh, show you all... uh, one of the loveliest pieces of ground... I found during my stay here near Ilfracombe. We should be going. Haunted, you know..."

⋙⋘

That was yesterday, I muttered to myself as I trudged up Torrs Walk and in this pre-dawn hour now stood before the entrance to another world. I now didn't hesitate to go up the path and past the gate posts. I hoped for a resolution. I prayed I would find a cottage. I knew in my heart I would not.

I instinctively reached for my magical coin and realized I had left it safely packed in my laptop case back at the hotel with the other coin Singh had given me; "The last one," as he had said. I had not shown it to anyone since literally stumbling upon it yesterday.

Finding it in the grass, where I had lost it on my first day here, was what allowed me the sanity I now possessed, and to recover for a pleasant remainder of the day with wife and friends. It went like this:

᠊ᡣ᠊ᢏ

After we had inspected the grounds, looked out over the sea, and I had described the magnificent Aurora Borealis, which by the way, Chief Constable White confirmed had been a nightly occurrence for the past week, we walked slowly back toward our cars.

It was just approaching full mid-day sun at this point. Somewhat tortured by this experience, but trying to put on the brave face, I asked if the others wouldn't please go ahead and give me a moment. Lingering behind about ten yards I pondered upon this scene, and gave my wife and friends the space they needed to quietly talk about how they were going to handle, "Jim, in his fragile emotional state."

As the others walked down the path, through the now wood gate, I walked around, attracted by a bright and shining object in the grasses. As I stepped forward my foot hit a rut of some kind, I tripped, but as I did my only thought was to reach for the coin. I grasped it, but remained laying there laughing. The others raced back concerned. I quickly and quietly stuffed it deeply into my trouser pockets, and literally giggled as a giddy child does at finding an important and long wished for present under the Christmas Tree.

As Mark reached down to help me up, I slowly raised to my feet realizing it was the first of the two medallions Singh had given me! *The one that fell from my pocket when I tripped with the bike that first day!*

"You okay, Jim?" Mark asked.

"Better than okay," I said. "I got this almost figured out. I feel like I just got part of my sanity back," I announced for everyone to hear.

Jeanne, visibly relieved, came over and gave me a hug. As we walked to the car I whispered, "It will all be okay now. Let's go have some fun today and then let's go home."

Arriving back at the hotel; I didn't want to lose this coin, my only link to mental and emotional equilibrium, I packed it with the other coin in the one piece of luggage Jeanne would also guard with her life – my laptop – the place I stored the writings that fed us and paid our bills.

Sunrise Present Day, Lamp Hill

I smiled, knowing something wonderful had indeed happened here over the past several weeks, and having the coin given to me by the mysterious Sikh from Punjab confirmed that. What that "something" was I now needed to find out. I'd play along with Jeanne and Mark and LaDawn's desire to help me get back home, functioning on all emotional cylinders. I'd just keep this new quest to myself.

I looked around me. The sun began to rise in the east and where light had shone through a guest room window to awaken me just the day before, now stood rubble; the same I found with Chief Constable White, wife, and friends. Though having the evidence of the lost coin, I still felt confused by it all.

Perhaps I was losing my mind. But then, the insane so often seem at perfect peace. I often felt that way – temporarily insane – mentally pushed against the tides of a modern world moving faster than my heart ever wanted to travel.

Confused though I was, my soul, did speak to me here. "He is real, Singh is real, and this place is just as his writing said, "*A return to innocence*," I voiced.

I wandered out back and found the oak tree by a boarded-over well, with other weathered boards lying scattered where I knew a tool shed once stood. I pulled up a seat and closed my eyes as my back leaned into the aged sentinel of Lamp Hill Lane. *I'm going fishing*, I thought. Scattered sunlight began to filter through the branches, scarred by time, but still boasting leafs.

What did he write? What did he say? I questioned myself. "Ah, yes," I replied to my own intellectual interrogatory. I smiled, closed my eyes and went back to his magnificent written lecture while whispering, "*We must daily seek a return to innocence, and when we do we will find 'the Privileged Place.'*"

34
THE PRIVILEGED PLACE

Surrendering to the sounds of rustling oak leaves, a gentle dawning of a new day, and the sound of the sea waves rhythmic crashing upon the nearby shores, I fell into the place I had come to believe was real, which no one else could see.

᪥

"Hello Singh," I said – my dreaming mind fully alert to this place I easily slipped into. He held out manuscript pages for me to read. I nodded, fully expecting him to simply disappear to the carriage and go wherever he did each day. Looking up from the pages, Singh had vanished, but the pages remained.

I turned them one by one and recognized them to be the same I had just finished making notes on, the day before yesterday. The magnificent, *"Principles of Power Thinking."* I seemed to know these by heart, and so, I set the pages on the grassy carpet beside me.

Though I knew I was asleep, the reality of the words penetrated my dream-consciousness and I reviewed each as if memorized. This was that "privileged place," a meditative, prayer-like location of the heart and mind which the mystery master of moral writings had taught me was available to anyone who should seek it.

I did come here with that intention, and exhausted, I carried on in both sleep and active dreamscape review. I heard once again another voice. This voice, the sacred one from my father said, "You have to go back son."

"How far back Dad?" I asked, remembering my dream of nights before.

"You'll know…"

So I tried to pick up the manuscript pages set down beside me, but a breeze picked them up and one by one carried them away. Out of my reach now, I focused upon memory; what I had read days before at our cottage *time machine*. As I mentally retrieved the words from the wise mystery author, they started to scroll before me, like lines appearing on a speaker's teleprompter do. *James* – the floating words began:

I offer you this first understanding in Power Thinking. "Nothing comes from nothing." As the poet Wadsworth said, "Our birth is but a sleep and a forgetting. The soul that rises with us, our life's star, hath elsewhere its setting and cometh from afar. Not in entire forgetfulness, and not in utter nakedness, but trailing clouds of glory, from God, who is our home."

These words then disappeared and I was left to ponder upon them. Once my meditative reflection was accomplished additional words appeared to view.

"Meaning and Potential" *is the first principle of Power Thinking. Just as there are two cre-*

ations in all things, you have had two creations. Your human ancestors gave you the genetic potential you possess, but your spirit DNA comes directly from God, who as Wadsworth declared "is our home." Many generations help make you who you are in physical form, but you are removed but one generation from the Great Creator! Together all the potential of a human and heavenly family resides within you! As was eloquently put forth in Dante's Divine Comedy: "Consider your origins. You were not formed to live like brutes, but to follow virtue and knowledge."

The realization of who you truly are, and the unlimited potential you possess, create the meaning, purpose and motivation to begin creating a new life. If you understand the full implication of your human and divine potential, and then do nothing else but pursue the truth of it, your life may be changed forever. If one wishes to continually build upon this first principle, then change and personal joy are limitless.

I was given time to ponder upon my own unlimited potential before new words came to view:

The "Heart and Mind Alliance" principle is second to understanding how to become a true "Power Thinker." It incorporates all the new meaning and purpose you have found in principle number one with a determined brain and heart alliance. Like-energy begets like-energy. Like thoughts beget like actions. If one wants permanent change he will listen to the voice of the heart as well as the head. Together with the potential found in principle one, the heart-mind energy exceeds all power output ever created.

Energy of the mind and heart must manifest itself in physical form if dwelled upon. "We think in secret, and it comes to pass… Environment is but our looking glass."

The words floated away and I expected some new wisdoms to appear. I waited. Not a word came. Then as I sat in vision-like slumber, the celestial dance of the previous several nights came to view. The Northern Lights, also called Aurora Borealis, dropped their curtain across the sky in panoramic display of dazzling colors more numerous than I could count, and in shades I could never describe. As the shimmering luminescence faded, words I had reviewed just days prior came again for me to read, as if on pages from the manuscript which had been carried away on the breeze. A soft voice read them to me this time:

The Power Think "Internalization" principle is the third and final of a truly Power Thinking lifestyle. Understanding truth is one thing, but "internalizing it" is to forever be partnered with it. In this ongoing process permanent change, peace, and joy is realized. We make a heaven on earth, and banish destructive forces of darkness from our minds forever.

To internalize anything, you must employ a pair of tools. First, you must "script" your life in advance. Much like a Three Act Play, a script for life will guide you, declare who you truly are, and give every detail of your vision for the ideal life. This "first creation" of your heart and mind will surely manifest itself in the physical world when you couple it with the second tool—the "Success M.A.P."

This MAP contains the three keys to greater self-mastery and real, lasting personal change. They are: Motive, Awareness, and Practice. They are most highly utilized in the "Privileged Place," that door to another world of learning and wonder… James…

As this voice died off, and realizing I was in a dream, I willed myself to stay there under the tree, enjoy the rest from more anxious days I had known. After some time of peace, and sound repose, another manuscript page floated back toward me. I reached out for it, but couldn't grasp it. I arose from my spot under the oak, and followed the page toward the edge of the property where a steep decline revealed the ocean below.

I heard the gentle voice again, but more audible now. It was the voice I had imagined being that of the mysterious owner of this estate on Lamp Hill Lane. It appeared to originate from the garden. I turned and followed it. In the garden, I walked to the tree and sat myself down again. Now in perfect awareness the voice added more to my heart.

It was a quiet and pleasant voice, but clear. *James,* it began:

One must decide to understand the principles of more powerful thinking by retreating from the noise and distractions of daily living. One must slow down to speed effectiveness in all things. This may occur when one enters the "Privileged Place." This personal island retreat may be visited any-time. We return to innocence of our child-like early years when we attend to this human need – a daily retreat from the incessant demands of life at light speed.

The "Privileged Place" does not demand perfection from us; it creates perfection within us. When we read, think quietly, and access the "ancient self" in a communion with the Holy Being of all creations, we begin our journey to create a newness and most power filled life. . . James . . .

"James? Sir? Mr. Pratt?" the voice gently probed. "Mr. Pratt, you have your family and friends here. They are worried," Chief Constable White said, as he carefully shook me awake.

I aroused from the pleasant dream and my eyes gradually focused upon Jeanne, whose sad-eye look spoke volumes. Mark tried to maintain a neutral, *"Hey buddy – How ya doin',"* look but he couldn't. LaDawn's expression showed pure compassion.

"Oh... Well. I just wanted to take a walk. Couldn't sleep. Thought if I came here one last time it would be good for me," I replied as I sleepily arose and brushed myself off. "What time is it?"

"Noon," Mark said.

"Wow! You guys are late sleepers. Sorry I put you through this once more. Perhaps we should be going; catch that last train out of Barnstaple for London, then home..." I said.

We all walked down the lane as I tried to show no emotion; be the good sport, but the place still tugged at me. I had again entered another world, even for a brief few hours. I knew I would never be the same. And my wife and friends?

I would have to share this with them in another way. I wasn't sure how I would do it, but I knew it was given to me by a Sikh, a mystery writer, and a cottage on Lamp Hill. They came into my head and heart as good muse's do for serious writers. And in essence they taught me this:

Each person has the right, and choice of leaving the noise and tumult behind. Each has the ability, if they seek it from within their very center, to find a special "privileged place," all of their own. There, on an island of sanity where they connect to their ancient self, a person may become whatever the heart desires. In the end man's purpose is to experience joy, peace, and love.

Lamp Hill Lane was going with me to Virginia. And would ever stay where it belonged – deep within my heart...

35
HYDE, SIKH, AND LEAVING ILFRACOMBE

I found our bags waiting in the lobby. The ladies set out to accomplish the official "check-out" and final billing matters while we all bid farewell to Chief Constable White. I was concerned about one other matter; the results from a note I had left in the pre-dawn hours with one James Hyde, Concierge.

I asked Mark if he would accompany me for a visit with this person now, who I was sure to be the same young man I had met but days before in the restaurant.

"Mark," I began as we went to visit the concierge. "If this is who I think it is, a lot of stuff will begin to make sense."

"Okay," came his simple reply.

The man's back was to us. My heart sunk. From the balding on the crown of his head, and portly figure, I knew we were dealing with someone else.

"Good day," he said with a smile, swiveling in his chair to meet us head on.

"How may I be of service?"

"You are Mr. Hyde, I presume?"

"Dr. Jekyll, actually," he said in good humored tone. "Depending upon the occasion," he continued playfully.

"Well, I was wondering about your name. That is, a few days ago, I…"

"You are the missing author! I have the note you left me right here," he said, holding it up. "Well I am sure glad to meet you! I just ordered your novels from an online store. May I get your autograph, sir?" He rummaged through his desk drawers and pulled out some stationary. "Oh, I do appreciate this, Mr. Pratt. My wife and I love reading a good fiction story," he finished.

I signed all five copies of stationary and wrote a note of "thanks" on one of them. "There you are, Mr. Hyde."

"Thank you!" he replied. "Now then, I cut you off. You were wondering about my name? In what way, sir?"

"My first day here in Ilfracombe I enjoyed dinner in your restaurant, and one of the waiters was named 'Jim Hyde.' Do you have a relative by the same name working here?"

"No sir. Quite odd. But that is interesting as questions go. I can't imagine how you would know of the anniversary, nor of the obscure history of the Hyde family working in the local hotel industry for three generations."

"Anniversary? Three generations?" I asked.

Mark and I had now taken seats before the man's desk and he led us through a history of the hotel, the family traditions of working here, and about one man and an anniversary celebrated each year by both hotel and Hyde family members.

"A 'Romeo and Juliet' romance of Victorian proportions really," he said. "She was of part Indian descent, and James Hyde was from a family which, I am proud to admit, mixed some two hundred years ago with a royal line, the Duke of Devon," he finished.

My mind raced and found itself scrolling through the *Hampton of Devon* story. I didn't give that connection away except for this: "Duke Cavandish?" I prompted.

"Why yes, Mr. Pratt. You know the family tree?"

"Well, sort of," I replied. "Dukes, Earls, they confuse me a bit... So," I continued as Mark took this all in, "that would explain the costumed party who had gathered that day last week in the restaurant, and one of your waiters playing the part of your great uncle, Jim Hyde?"

He returned my questions with a quizzical expression. "We celebrate it on the fourth week of the month. Tonight in fact. Your visit started three weeks ago? Did it not?"

I didn't want to go there. I kept my silence.

"Do you have the date of the supposed accident?" Mark asked. "The betrothal date of young Jim and fiancé' from your family history?" Mark added.

James Hyde arose and gestured for us to follow. He led us to the photo gallery section of the hallway leading to rooms on the first level. He pointed to an aged photo. "Here is the photo of a group of young employees. The date October 8, 1911. Taken that morning, just by chance. In this photo," he continued, pointing to the next, "is the betrothal party seated at tables off the veranda, right over there." He pointed past the table I had been seated at in the restaurant my first day here.

I examined the photo carefully. I recognized the face of the young man, and several of the costumed party members.

"You say this photo is nearly 100 years old?"

"Yes sir, Mr. Pratt."

I looked closer. In the back of the party dressed in turn of the century outfits was the blurred image of a taller man, bearded and wearing something I now blurted out with excitement for all to hear, "A turban!"

36
GONE FISHING

I remained quiet for the entire return trip to the states. The photo of Singh with the waiter Jim Hyde, and no one to answer my seeming reason for recognizing them was just more ammunition for those thinking I could use a visit with the men in "white coats."

I was determined to put it all behind me. Besides, if I was crazy I was pleasantly surprised by it all. *Could a trip have been more interesting?* I asked myself over and over. *Why should I expect them to understand?* I mused, in consideration of what Jeanne, Mark, and LaDawn experienced. *They can't understand what they can't explain. Then how can I?* I reasoned as the British Airways jet pulled in to the terminal at Dulles.

I was immediately met outside the airport by reporters who had followed my story of disappearance in England. "I'll supply answers when I can write out what I have been through," I simply replied.

Mark shielded me, and even got a taxi to get us away from the lights, cameras, and crowds seeking answers. The taxi ride was short – all the way to "Long Term Parking" where my car required an airing out from the canine episode weeks before.

Off the airport property we stopped, got some cleaner and air freshener, and I began to explain in more detail the obstacles that seemed to plague me in getting to England in the first place.

"This entire trip has been strange," I opened up as we drove home to Lexington, where Mark and LaDawn would spend the night before heading on to a speaking engagement in Raleigh.

I recounted the stray bullet flying into the windshield, the temporary arrest at Dulles for gun powder residue on my hands, the police doggie doing his sniffing then soiling of my car seat, the Central Park drug bust incident and what I called "...the JFK airport cousin-to-Singh '*In the center you will find dee way*!' story."

"Quite a tale!"

"That's what I do," I responded dryly.

"I have been meaning to ask though; 'What happened to *Hampton of Devon*?'" Mark probed.

"His ship sunk, somewhere off the coast at Ilfracombe."

"And the story? I mean what did you write about? All that time... You must have put something on paper. I know you pretty well, Jim," Mark pushed.

Jeanne looked over at me with a questioning glance, and I winked back. She was concerned that I still might become "pushed over the edge," so to speak. I answered Mark simply about my writing.

"More than you can know. More than anyone might believe. It was so incredible that if it all was just a delusion, I have never learned, felt, and drunk so deeply regarding what thoughts once *internalized* in the heart may actually become."

I knew something about Mark. I could look at him and sense things. Most often his furrowed brow, while indicating deep thought, also indicated deep compassion. Mark has never been about money, just about people.

"Jim," he began carefully. "That hilltop property with the crumbled brick and stone overlooking the sea near Ilfracombe became a sanctuary, of sorts, with incalculable meaning for you."

"Yes," I simply replied.

"Jim," Mark added. "I personally will make you a promise. I will check out that property's chain of ownership back as far as it goes."

I thanked Mark and for the remainder of the drive through the Shenandoah Valley to Lexington we made small talk, some Civil War history lessons, talked of Jeanne's enjoyment, and mine, of remodeling our ante-bellum home in Rockbridge County. Some good Southern-style faith was brought up, and the topic of mind and body science touched upon too; Mark's specialty.

I promised to take Mark fishing early in the morning. "General Robert E. Lee's secret fishing hole," I assured with a grin.

"Uh oh," Jeanne allowed. "Jim, you promised to swear off story-telling for a while."

"But it's true and..."

"Ah! Just stop," she gently scolded. "You need to just 'go fishing' like normal people do. Just go fishing honey, and try to leave the stories behind. It will be good for you."

Some laughter accompanied my promise to Jeanne, and I wondered how I could accomplish it. "So, what's a delusional writer to do for fun while he's fishing? No one will believe me when I get home with 'the big one that got away' story, even if it's true," I said.

Take a break and get my mind off telling tales, was the advice my wife and friends were giving. So Mark and I went fishing and rafting down the Shenandoah.

Weeks went by. I hadn't touched my laptop. Didn't read the journal I sent via Fed Ex from England. Didn't look for the medallion I had carefully hidden in a zipper pouch in the lap top bag... I just needed some time. Something apparently lost from me.

I read a few books with no other agenda other than simple pleasure. Jeanne and I took a quick trip out west to give the worried kids a hug. Mark was coming back to town tomorrow for a speaking engagement at Southern Virginia University. I was still scheduled for the lecture promised weeks ago, "Life is a Three Act Play," up at Virginia Military Institute this afternoon, and was starting to get the writing itch again, but...

Promises... I promised Jeanne to stay away from my keyboard for a couple of months, just be "normal" and finish the remodel we had started. She was sure the physical therapy would soothe the over-active mind, and I had to agree.

I had taken a new interest in gardening, and though late in the planting season had determined to till an acre, add soil amends, and get ready for spring planting. Whatever I had experienced in England did have an affect on me with regards to touching base with the earth, reflection through hard physical work, and enjoying a slowness I had not allowed myself to enjoy for several years.

So there I am, fixing fence posts for a corral which, I promised, would soon hold two of Jeanne's wandering pet alpacas and one flower chewing llama, when I received a phone call on my cell.

"Hello?"

Static.

"Hello?"

A scratchy voice sounded but was unclear.

"Hello… I can't hear you. Hello?"

"James… a promise… …Bookery in…"

Static.

"Hello? Anybody there?"

My heart pounded louder than the static, louder than the barely audible voice in the cell phone. I put my hands on my head and paced. I wanted this to stop – or be finished with. *I need to get a job… Forget this entire writing business,* I muttered to my alpaca and llama friends tied up nearby. One snorted. The other spit in reply. "My sentiments, exactly," I said.

I had to respond to this. Bury the experience and get on with life, but as "Dad" often reminded me, there is no way "around" most things, just "through." I opened my cell phone to see if the "Received Calls" feature had stored the strange call.

"Private Number," I replied to my own question. "Okay. Well then… VMI is still on the schedule. I think I'll stop by The Bookery while in Lexington. Probably a call from the store manager," I assured my rapidly beating heart. "Probably a book I ordered…" I added to my mind on hyper-ventilate.

I left the tools in the field, and decided I would digress from my promise to Jeanne, (to stay away from book stores and the business,) just for this afternoon. After that, I'd go back to fence posts, and then do as my mysterious English wizard had instructed; continue *fishing…*

37
The Book... Again

I enjoyed the speaking engagement at VMI. I had disconnected from my speech giving for many weeks, and I even thought I could be content by simplifying my life. But my topic, *Life is a Three Act Play*, meant even more to me now, since *Hampton of Devon's* author, had eluded me.

My manager Maryann had, along with the rest of the country, become aware of my "missing in Ilfracombe" for three weeks due to the cable news shows, and the BBC contacting her, and she too suggested I take a month, or two, or three, off... Basically, I was to "chill out" and allow things to "cool off" so she could go back fresh to New York and engage the interest of her literary agent contact again. Agents and publishers don't mind eccentric authors, but they don't want crazy ones. Crazies have trouble delivering manuscripts.

So, what could it hurt answering the mystical cell phone clues; the promptings to go into Lexington and visit The Bookery? I was just as sure as anyone that I was hearing things. So this little stop and a pleasant visit with the owner couldn't hurt, only help me touch base with reality.

"Hello?" I called out as I entered the store. *Strange. 4:00 pm and no one in the store,* I mused. "Hello!" I called a bit louder. Still no one, so I wandered to the back of the store. *Maybe a meeting or book-signing back here,* I thought.

The Bookery on Nelson Street specializes in rare, used, signed, Civil War, collectibles, out-of-print, classics, along with a variety of titles from local authors. Coming in here makes me feel sane, as if I'm connected to other dreamers who risked time and energy to communicate on paper their deepest thoughts and knowledge.

I enjoy passing by the racks of aged books and as I moved toward the back, I almost forgot my purpose in coming here.

"Hello, Mr. Pratt," a cheerful and familiar female voice called, but not one associated with the employees. In fact, the entire store layout seemed changed since I had last been in here before my trip to England.

"Miriam?" I asked. "Is that you?"

"Yes sir, Mr. Pratt. And I have a book for you," she added cheerily. She stepped behind an aged wood crafted counter, one I had not recalled seeing before, and reached below to a shelf. "Here you are, Mr. Pratt. I do hope you enjoy it," she added.

"Well... I don't know what to say. First, what are you doing here, and why all the changes?"

"Well, I am back from school, and my god-mother needed a bit of help, as we are closing down soon. Illness in the family," she finished.

"Oh, I am sorry to hear that. I didn't know the store was closing. How sad. And your god-mother? I thought all family and relations were in England..." I felt a bit confused at this point. "The last I saw you was at the Lee Chapel. We walked and talked and I left you with…"

"Two chapters from *Hampton of Devon*," she interjected.

"Yes. The beginning to the story," I replied. "Have you enjoyed it?"

"Very much, Mr. Pratt. I think you will too."

I looked down at the strange packaging of the book now in my hands; simple brown wrapping paper tied in a bundle with string, with a note attached in elegant cursive, but with a feminine flair. I looked back up to remark about this to Miriam. "This is quite unique. Tell your god-mother that I…"

"What was that?" the student age store-clerk answered, from behind the glass case.

"Hey, where did Miriam… What happened to the wood counter? I got this book… Who are you?" I nervously demanded.

"Are you okay, sir?" she replied. "You don't look so good. Do you need help?" the young woman asked.

"I didn't come into this…" I posed. "This is different," I added in a somewhat concerned voice; borderline panic really. "I… I… I've got to go!" I said, and then hurried toward the street exit.

Passing by several customers, still clutching the wrapped parcel with note attached, I looked frantically up and down Nelson Street. Up on the hill was Washington and Lee and the Lee Chapel, adjacent to VMI from where I had just come.

I started toward the Lee Chapel, drawn to it, knowing something my mind didn't understand but my heart pounded with. I picked up my pace and then started jogging toward it, my eyes darting around in search of Miriam. If I was going crazy, whatever I had in this package would have to help me through it. Whoever she really was would have to become explained.

I reached the ground, out of breath, and searched the chapel's exterior for any sign of her. I turned to go back toward the front on 11 University Place, the road leading up to VMI from Lee. I was becoming very familiar with these grounds.

Regaining my breath, and realizing I was chasing a phantom, I sat down on a bench in the shade of a stately pine to examine my mental state; and the package securely held in my right hand. I wasn't letting go of this. It was sanity in physical form. It was, in short, handed to me by someone who knew something about me; enough to reach me on my cell phone and prompt me back to the delusional realm of fancy from which I had just escaped weeks ago.

I played with the string, unsure if I should even open it here. *I need to show this to Jeanne. Get someone to see me open the thing.* But the string tugged at my heart, and not at my head. I slipped the string off the rough brown exterior and pulled the packaging paper back.

Staring back at me was the cover of a book I had seen weeks before. *The one I had told Mark Kastleman about… On a cell phone call from Ilfracombe!*

My fingers trembled with unsteady hands as I turned the aged pages carefully. I somehow knew what I was going to find, and the dots I could not connect for weeks became clear; this was not only the author of the most treasured book on thought and action, the granddaddy to all self-improvement books and the inspiration to over fifty million readers for more than one hundred years, this was the man who I had studied from at Lamp Hill Lane!

My heart raced as I reached the title page. My business card with the note I had written upon the back requesting this book, fell to the floor. I reached down for it. Misty-eyed, I wasn't crazy, and yet this couldn't be…

Why here? Why now? I asked, with emotion gripping my mind. Salty moisture obscured my clear view of the handwritten signature so elegantly penned in the cursive I had come to know.*

I hurriedly re-wrapped the book in the paper. I would read the note attached to this package at my desk back home. I had other things; things untouched which I had brought back with me from England, that now needed my attention.

I stopped only briefly to see out from the corner of my eye, the white entry door to Lee Chapel closing, and behind it someone who had suddenly appeared there. She smiled, waved cheerily, and then disappeared into the sacred haunt.

I thought for the briefest moment of following her inside, then simply smiled, internalizing all that was happening. I knew what I had to do. There was a magical medallion to find, writings from the mystery man, and perhaps the answers to the identity of the author of *Hampton of Devon* had been here, at home in Lexington, all along. It was all becoming clear to a troubled mind; one my dearest family and friends had worried over. I had evidence of my travel to another place and time. I had the book!

38
Time Machine

I didn't allow the copy of this rare autographed book out of my hands, except for the ride home. Then I made sure it sat on my lap. I was sure if it disappeared, if I couldn't physically feel it in my possession, I would need some rest, the kind associated with psychological rehabilitation programs at quasi-hospital retreats – you know, for the emotionally disturbed, somewhere in the Poconos.

Like an addict who needed just "one drink" I had slipped in to town, downed a few literary shots found in a lecture and at a bookstore, got a little tipsy, and then got a gift book from a ghost.

What's so unusual about that? I questioned, as I considered Jeanne's insistence I stay away from the creative writing for a few months.

I pulled in to the drive happy to see Jeanne had returned from shopping. I had this treasure, evidence of my sanity to share with her. The story still had a ways to go – just to work the kinks out – but gradually the seeming loss of time in England, where I stayed, who I saw, what I did, how I felt, would all blend into a believable and seamless story of inspiration that she could believe... *Wouldn't she?*

৵৽৵৻

"Hi honey," I called.

She walked up from the mailbox with a questioning look on her face. "Jim? What is this?" she asked, holding up a letter to me.

"Let's see," I answered, holding the book securely under my arm and against my side. I took the letter from her hands and smiled. "Wow!"

"What?" she asked.

"I can hardly believe..." I didn't finish. I turned it over, saw the post mark, and then pulled the book out from under my arm.

"Hey! Jim! Where are you going?" she called as I took several leaps toward the surround porch, disappearing into the bowels of the remodel.

I hurried to my 1900 era antique roll-top desk. I laid the book and the letter with the out-of-date post mark upon the desk. I believed something would happen here. I recalled all the time spent on Lamp Hill, my search for *Hampton of Devon's* author, and what the constable said about the cottage, destroyed by fire in 1918. "*'There was one thing that miraculously survived,'* Constable White said."

"Jim, what on earth are you mumbling about? What is so important? You are worrying me," Jeanne offered as she slowly came up behind me.

I held my hand up and continued to focus. Jeanne knew what this meant. It was our sign that I had to stay on mental track, and for her not to be offended. She retreated to another room. It most often happened while my fingers were flying on the keyboard, lost in thought. But now my mind focused upon this desk, and my hands lifted the Olympia typewriter up to look beneath it.

"Oh my... This can't... I don't..." I have a bad habit of not finishing sentences when excited. I was extremely so now. I felt under the typewriter. "It's there!" I yelled out.

"What's there?" Jeanne called back, a bit frustrated.

"Honey," I said. "Please take this."

She returned to my side. I handed her the letter. I then set the typewriter aside. "Please open it. It's addressed to you. I want you to see with your own eyes what I've been trying to tell you. I have to check this desk out."

She nodded, scrunched her face quizzically, and took the letter with her to the nearby love-seat.

I then examined the wood desk-top more carefully. *The scratch,* I muttered as I ran my right hand over it again and again. I dropped from the seat and now knelt on the floor. I next examined the desk legs carefully. *These too,* I spoke softly. Then I looked up underneath the desk, examining the bottom side of the center drawer and desk built-ins.

I was more than just a bit animated. "This is it! Good heavens, Jeanne! This is it! This is the desk I worked at! This is... my time machine!"

She interrupted, "Jim? Oh, my. Jim... Do you know what you said here?"

"Huh," I was giddy. Laughing, teary eyed, joyous, feeling reborn, and definitely *not* crazy. "Honey, do you know what I have here?" I answered with an outstretched hand pointing to the desk.

"Jim. You better read this," she said, patting the seat next to her. I happily plopped myself beside her and picked up the letter. I had forgotten what I had written. I read it now.

I looked at Jeanne. She looked at me.

I smiled. "So – am I crazy, or sane?" I asked.

Her reply was simple, hand over mouth, and questioning eyes as she whispered, "Oh my..."

39
POST MARK, 1911

"*Dear Jeanne*," the letter sent from Ilfracombe with the 1911 postmark began.

I am safe, though strange forces seem at work since I left home days ago. I expect to call from my cell phone soon. The nightly Northern Light display plays havoc with transmission and reception; the magnetic fields interrupt electronic signals. I am staying the weekend at a cottage outside of Ilfracombe. No running water, just an 1800's manufactured hand pump, an out-house, no electricity; all as if time has stood still for one hundred years. I am enjoying the simplicity and the serenity of this hill-top bed and breakfast on Lamp Hill Lane over-looking the Atlantic, despite these inconveniences.

"I found an original copy of a book I have been wanting forever. You know the one. Simply look upon my desk for my 1972 copy. This edition is an original and it is signed!

"Thank you for letting me come here; for the trust you showed. I know I am supposed to be here. I have the strangest feeling that this trip will result in the magic of a new book, but even more, something whispers to me that it will become life changing; for us, for our friends — and perhaps for readers around the world.

I thought a real letter, with a real post mark, instead of emails, would be old-fashioned romantic! Sending love with all my heart... Jim

She had snuggled close to me. Then I unfolded and read an attached note:

Dear Postal Customer. It is with profound regret that this letter, postmarked 1911 from Ilfracombe, Devon, England, had been misplaced by the USPS. We can only assume the sender and addressee may be deceased. It was found along with other mail and items we hope you, as surviving relatives or next of kin, may help us deliver. If you would kindly visit our Lexington, Virginia Post Office branch, these items will be shown to you for identifying purposes. The United States Post Office regrets the human error and mishandling causing the delay in receipt of this letter and the contents of the package associated with it.

"Sincerely, Postmaster," I read aloud.

"Well, they got part of it wrong," Jeanne said.

"Which part?" I asked.

"The sender isn't deceased."

"Jeanne..." I began. "I sense after this trip and now with this, and the full tale I haven't shared that..."

I stopped, got up, looked out the window from my office to the woods beyond, wondered how to say what I was feeling. After all, I experienced something that now had ample evidence to support it; I could prove things others claimed I could not have experienced.

"Jim? What is it? You sense what?" Jeanne tenderly probed.

I turned to face her; motioned for her to come to my old English writing desk. I sat on the chair as she spontaneously sat on my lap. We uncovered the gift book together which I had just received from Miriam at The Bookery. I pointed at the message inside the book and then the signature.

She gasped, and tears formed. She knew of my love for this philosopher, and that I owned nearly twenty copies of his public domain work, created in print by as many different publishers. My original copy, given me by my mother in my 19th year, had sat on every desk I ever owned during 30 years of marriage, to remind me "how thoughts" affect life's actions and thus also life's circumstances.*

I finally formed the words to answer her question, and it was this: "Jeanne... I sense that time and even death are not what they seem to be, but then perhaps neither is living..."

40
The Package

"Slow down. You'll get us killed before we find out what is in the package!"

"If I slow down, they'll close. These people are government employees. They may not deliver mail on time but they do close on time."

She closed her eyes. I smiled. I wasn't going *that* fast; well maybe a tad over the 55 mile per-hour speed limit. Jeanne definitely thinks I take too many chances, but I wasn't going to spend a sleepless night wondering what was in the package referred to by the Post Master. Neither was she.

We hadn't lingered long after reading the note when we realized forty minutes remained until Lexington's Post Office would be closing for the day. It would take thirty minutes hitting lights just right.

Jeanne had decided to bring the prized copy of the original 1902 book given to me by the vanishing Miriam. I spent the remainder of our travel to town discussing Miriam's appearance at the Chamber of Commerce event, her disappearance in the Lee Chapel, her appearance again in The Bookery, and her vanishing once again into the Lee Chapel.

"How do you explain her?"

"You wouldn't believe me," I answered.

"I don't know what to believe… or what not to, anymore. Why do so many weird and unusual things happen to you? I don't know anyone who has the number of unexplainable adventures, sightings of vanishing people, false arrests, loss of time, stories falling in their laps; and I'm just getting warmed up," Jeanne said.

"You mean I'm not normal?" I asked with a grin.

She just laughed and looked out the window to the passing countryside. "Jim, maybe you are normal, but what happens when you go on the hunt for a story definitely is not."

"Honey – there is a difference in 'hunting for a story' and scripting one in advance."

"What?"

"I've learned over the past year of chasing Hampton's ghostwriter that it wasn't mere chance that made the story appear."

"I don't follow. It came off the Internet and then disappeared. Like falling in your lap," she answered.

"No sweetheart. I was looking for a story I could love and embrace. *Hampton of Devon* didn't appear out of effortless searching. It may appear some serendipitous good fortune simply smiled upon me, but an average effort won't do for this kind of work. You have to be constantly creating a premise and set up beliefs for ACT I in your activities while anticipating complications; ACT II stuff. If you write your own 'life-script' in advance, the victories take care of themselves. I'll find *Hampton of Devon* and its author. You just watch."

"It still seems strange."

"That's the point. Scripting a novel or play is about suspending disbelief in one thing and creating belief in another. If people understood that, they could literally recreate their lives. Hampton's author did that for me."

"So what happens now?"

"We keep our eyes open. We watch for hints, clues, listen to intuitions. Let me give you some examples how that can work..."

I then shared every single event and clue I could think of that led me upon the journey across the sea and finally back home to where it all began.

"Nothing comes from nothing," I offered. "Ex Nihilo Nihil fit."

"Since we came home from England, you've used that one a lot. Why?"

"Because there was so much I couldn't explain. Yet everything that is or will be, has a beginning. It's simply a matter of following the dots and then connecting them. Right here," I said. "My *time machine* – it has every evidence pointing to it being in a fire. It has a chain of ownership to an auction house in London. These are facts. Believing that it is the one from my fanciful stay at the cottage I alone appear to have experienced, may be an over-worked mind playing tricks on me. Maybe it all was just a dream.

"But what about the book from the girl Miriam, this package, and all the rest," Jeanne asked.

I smiled. She posed it as if almost self-talk. She was starting to be open.

"Here, look at this." I pulled from my coat pocket a plastic bag and in it was the medallion Singh had given me. I handed it to her.

Jeanne examined it. "Ex Nihilo Nihil Fit," she read. "Okay, I get that."

"Turn it over," I said.

"Ex Tempore," she read. "This is a beautiful etching. The profile of a man with the light coming up from behind him and the words 'Thought' on one side and 'Power' on the other."

"Look closely under the man's profile," I instructed.

"I can't read it. I'd need a magnifying glass."

"I needed one too when I first noticed it. It reads 'Ex Animo.'"

"So 'Tempore?'"

"Most translations agree it is rendered, 'In consequence of time,'" I answered.

"Ex Animo?"

"In the heart," I replied.

"Where did you get this?" she followed.

"From Singh."

There was silence for the remainder of our trip into Lexington. Jeanne played with the coin, turning it over and over and not sure what to make of it. I was tempted to explain how the mystical Sikh had greeted me at the gate on Lamp Hill, and how this coin became my "entrance fee," but let it alone.

Her wheels were turning. I knew she wasn't sure if I had told her everything, but indeed I had... except about this entrance token to another world.

"Here we are. What time do you have?" I asked as we pulled up curbside to the stately Federal Post Office building on the corner of Lee and Nelson.

"Four fifty-six. You got four minutes."

"Come on," I urged.

"I'll stay with the car. You hurry. Go!" she insisted.

I nodded, smiled, raised my eyebrows, and raced up the steps to get inside just as the Post

Office was closing.

I went to the Post Master's office, knocked on the door, and was greeted by, exactly, no one. "Hello? Anyone? Hello?" I probed gently as I put my foot inside the office. I looked around and found the office empty. I could hear voices in the back just beyond this office but no one appeared to my call.

I turned to leave, then a box caught my eye. Upon the desk was a note on standard postal stationary. It read: *This box for Mr. James Pratt, heirs, or closest relative.*

I picked it up and went outside the office to the counter. The door shut behind me. "Strange," I mumbled.

I walked around the corner to the lobby as the lights turned out along with the "Closed" signs offered upon the counter. The lobby stayed open for post box customers and I looked for anyone who might be in authority to make sure I was not doing anything illegal by taking this box out of the building.

"The post office is now closed. We will open promptly at 8:00 am tomorrow. Thank you for your patronage," a recording offered.

Options… *Well – can't take it back. Guess I'll sign for it tomorrow.* I managed to act normal while noticing the security cameras positioned upon the upper corners of the lobby. I left the lobby and jogged down the steps and met Jeanne waiting for me.

"You got it!" she excitedly said. "Let's open it!"

"Hold on. Not so quick. This was too easy. Something must be wrong."

"What?"

"Nobody greeted me. Just the box on the Post Master's desk with my name on it. I couldn't just leave it there, so I took it. But I should go back in the morning to sign a release."

"Ugh!"

"You really want to see what's in here don't you!" I laughed.

"This is easy for you, Jim. This kind of stuff doesn't happen to us 'normal' people everyday. I want to see what is inside!" she complained, like a child examining her wrapped birthday present before the party begins.

"You're disappointed," I noted as we pulled out and headed for home.

"Jim. What's in this box?"

"I don't know. A bomb?"

"Really! You must have some idea!" she protested.

"My little voice tells me we should simply go home, snuggle up to the fire and read the gift book I was given today. We should sort that one out first. Then if we really can't make it until tomorrow, we'll open this box. I can always sign for it and prove my identity."

"Promise?"

"Jeanne! This is the new you. You are becoming a believer!"

"Well, I'm curious and this last month has given me a lot to think about; almost losing you, watching you go through all the doubts, and I know…" She stopped abruptly in mid-sentence.

"You know what?" I asked as we neared the state highway.

She seemed genuinely touched. "Jim, you think with your heart. I always knew that about you, but I thought you maybe were just a little too much on the 'feely' side of things, and didn't stop to analyze things enough. I'm starting to see some things from your point of view."

"Keep that thought." I reached in my trouser pocket for my coin just to make sure it was there. I smiled, winked and knew that what was becoming normal for me was becoming expected by my wife. This rare book, mystery coin, and now ancient package were headed to their Virginian home, where an Englishman's desk awaited them.

41
"Where Your Treasure Is…"

We had stopped at one of our favorite country diners, enjoyed a hearty meal and seemed to savor the promise of something inside a book and a box. We let neither out of our sight, taking them inside with us.

For some reason we decided not to go directly home. We drove through Rockbridge County enjoying the late afternoon autumn coming on to trees and foliage, and made our way to the Blue Ridge Mountains and back home to the valley by nightfall.

We spent hours pouring over our past, the difficult parts of thirty years of life and marriage, the happy parts too. Both of us had been near death on more than one occasion, but spared. Both of us had suffered mental and emotional torments but by the literal grace of God, healed. We had watched loved ones travel roads of pain, and were not able to stop them from it. Friends and family passed away. Five decades and the saddest of the life-storms passed through, now found us finally in calm seas. We marveled at it all.

We contemplated upon the way the world and its inhabitants had sped up from our youthful days of vinyl records, electric typewriters, wall mounted telephones, and classic cars to seek more of something; what that something was, we weren't able to identify exactly. To the world-wise there always seemed to be something else on the horizon to reach, grasp for, need, want, or have in order to feel "successful."

"More stuff," Jeanne said.

"Less contentment," I added.

I loved the growing innocence and simplicity in my wife. She grew more so with age, and the more she did, the more beautiful she was to me. I never understood how old men could love their old wives so much; when I was young, and in a hurry, and had no thought of life ending, and the aging-wrinkles meant exhaustion to me and not beauty blended with light and wisdom. How foolish and what a shame it is that the splendor of youthful energy, and its full vigor are spent in pursuits to have more stuff.

"Funny how that is," I supplied as we entered the driveway. Jeanne nodded in agreement, with a yawn of exhaustion.

"Are you going to read to me?" she asked.

"Yes, I am."

"Good. I want to rest listening to your voice. I'm afraid one of these days I'll wake up and you'll be gone."

"Why is that?"

"I think you like 1911 better."

I didn't say anything; just smiled as I opened the car door for her.

We grabbed our things, greeted our faithful Labrador, Sugar, who followed us inside, tail going at second-hand clock speed. Jeanne lit the fire in the study and pulled out a comforter.

Sugar relaxed at her feet. We placed the slightly crumpled, but definitely aged gift box upon the desk. I pulled the coin from my pocket and placed it on top.

"Ready?" I asked.

"Uh huh," she answered, head upon my shoulder.

I read. This small 1902 original copy of the classic tome on the effects of thought and circumstance took but one hour to read aloud. I finished with the final paragraph:

"Tempest tossed souls, wherever you may be, under whatsoever conditions you may live, know this— In the ocean of life the isles of blessedness are smiling, and the sunny shore of your ideal awaits your coming. Keep your hand firmly upon the helm of thought. In the ship of your soul reclines the commanding master. He does but sleep. Awake him!"

I looked over to Jeanne. She was asleep. Along with these words her warmth assured me that whatever storm may yet come, we are indeed, with God at the center, masters of thought, masters of circumstance, and whatever came our way in life, we could handle it together.

I allowed her to have the love seat, covered her, and went to my desk to contemplate the contents of the mystery package. My bible was upon the desk top and opened. I didn't recall putting it there.

"Speak to me," I said as I pulled it up to my eyes to find the magical final verse before retiring. My eyes fell easily upon the right hand page, middle of the out-side column. I looked over once more to the wife I married thirty years ago and smiled as I contemplated upon this day with her, and all we were still discovering together. The verse from St. Matthew 6:21 said it all: *For where your treasure is, there will your heart be also.*

42
THE PROMISE

I left early enough to not disturb Jeanne. She seemed exhausted from the discussion and ideas that I had proposed to her – that perhaps I had experienced something ethereal, extraordinary, and yet very tangible while losing myself in Ilfracombe exactly thirty days ago.

Arriving to the Lexington Post Office, I inquired at the Post Master's office regarding the package. I explained picking it up the day before, the door locking behind me, the postal clerk windows becoming suddenly closed, and said that I came to remedy the situation; to sign a release for the package.

The Post Master was quite congenial, but she stated that in no way had she left her door ajar, opened, or had ever seen the package tucked under my arm.

"Well someone else must have put it there," I answered.

"Please excuse me, Mr. Pratt. I'll just poke around and find out who may have some information regarding your package. Please have a seat."

I took the seat and examined the tired looking box carefully. It was rectangular, the size of a ream of paper, and had that musty smell that something stored in an attic for decades acquires.

"Mr. Pratt," she said upon returning. "I apologize for the delay. Are you sure, sir, that you got this package from my office?"

I didn't answer directly. I knew where this was headed. "Perhaps I am thinking of something else. Perhaps between my wife and I there is some confusion."

"Well, Mr. Pratt… we have no record of the delivery being made through our office," she finally spoke.

"Good day then, and thank you for the trouble."

She scrunched her face in a reply which meant, "You need help," then forced a smile.

Used to the reaction, I tipped the brim of my ball cap, and exited; package under arm. I wasn't sure how I would explain this to Jeanne, but then decided "Why even try?" I got in my car and sped home, eager to unlock the mystery inside, with Jeanne at my side.

It was overcast, and a heavy downpour began to make the driving hazardous. At one point I pulled over and wondered if I should simply wait out the storm, find out what was inside the box, and then call Jeanne and tell her about it.

Almost as suddenly as it began, the Shenandoah Valley thunderstorm broke and the clouds parted. A glorious rainbow appeared in the west towards which I drove.

In all my years I had never found the "end of the rainbow." As elusive as holding on to a raindrop from the storm preceding its appearance, the rainbows I have witnessed were far off. Like a holographic image you could not quite touch, they contained a multi-colored promise; the Sunday School lesson kind reminding the children of men that a Noah-like flood would never happen again. I thought on that now as I found myself actually entering the end of this rainbow. I was stunned to be under it. The child in me looked in the pastures for the leprechaun and pot of gold.*

I immediately stopped the car, and took in this prism-filtered light show. I sensed the promise to me personally, that the floods of past doubt, past sorrows, and past frustrations were just that; passed through, over, completed and that this new life with Jeanne, my writing, and discoveries would lead to more than personal healing. I then realized it was thirty days exactly since I had returned home from Ilfracombe. I wondered about that as I turned to get back into my car.

I paused. I thought I heard his voice, a gentle sigh upon the breeze. It wafted through the painter's palette poured on the air around me, dissipating as the rainbow hues evaporated. Unless it was just vivid imaginings, this ghost whisperer reminded me of a promise he made to me while staying at a cottage on Lamp Hill. It was this:

"When your thirty days are finished, you will know me."

43
The Secret

I arrived home midday. Jeanne was standing outside waiting. Worried, she had placed several calls.

"Forgot to take my cell phone. Sorry, sweetheart," I said.

"Well?" she posed.

"A dead end," I replied simply. "Kind of chilly. Let's start a fire." I explained the Post Master's response as we went inside. I laid the box upon the desk top and we both just stood there uncertain whether to open it or call the Rockbridge County Sheriff's Bomb Squad.

"You mean no one knew where it came from?"

"Well, it does say Ilfracombe, post marked 1911. If it explodes we die together. Should we go... You know... Have one last... Fling?" I finally teased with a tilt of my head towards the staircase.

"Would you please just open it! I haven't been able to think of anything else all morning."

I obliged and carefully undid the string first, then carefully cut away one end of the rectangular box with a razor knife. Our heads lightly butted as we both eagerly peered inside.

"Paper," she said.

"Ah... not just paper love, but ink," I said. "Drum roll?"

"Please just pull the stack of papers out," she ordered.

I smiled and obeyed.

As the two inch thick document came to light, I noticed the familiar handwriting I had not seen since spending time upon Lamp Hill. "This is his," I simply stated.

"Whose?" she asked.

"The Lamp Hill estate owner. The mystery writer," I answered.

Jeanne didn't ask any more questions. Like a magnet drawing us to the sofa in the den where a fire warmed the room, and with the cracking and boom of thunderheads making this afternoon once again dark and ominous, the setting became a spontaneous sanctuary from the storm, but appropriate for a mystery novel. We sat close and began to read the cover letter. I acted as voice while Jeanne read along:

Dear Mr. Pratt,

As promised, and because of your belief in me, I enclose the final manuscript written after your careful review of my daily scribbling which you so capably edited and without which I would have never ventured to offer to the world. I had told you that you would come to know me by the end of your thirty day trip. Upon reading this finished manuscript I believe you shall.

"Signed, *Your servant and friend in Ilfracombe,*" I read.

What happened next was a blur of time spent in nearly two hundred handwritten pages of immaculate penmanship. Jeanne didn't move for the many hours it took to read.

We marveled at the wisdom, and I stopped every few pages and recalled to her my impressions when I had first read these words. But this was expanded upon and deeper, and Victorian, and unusual, and wholly out of the realm of anything I might be able to produce. I had to make sure Jeanne understood this was genuine material; not some silly ruse or game. So, in addition to the time it took to read this document many hours of discussion were added.

It wasn't hard to get lost in discussion, for we had to stop and let what we were reading settle in. The depth of feeling found in the passages about thought, action, meaning, purpose, motives, awareness, practices, light, love, and choices we make was, in a word; profound. These pages required digesting, and not hurried reading.

We didn't sleep, didn't eat, and by morning we laid the final page aside, stunned at the magnitude of what was contained in the cursive style of a master philosopher. "Honey – listen to this," I said. "The final paragraph of the manuscript says it all: *These heart-minded laws and principles, of which I have shed light upon, I shall refer to as Power Thinking.*

"He said I'd get to know him at the end of thirty days. I know him now. I even think if he didn't tell me his name I would be right," I said.

"Who are you thinking the writer is?" Jeanne asked.

"The same who wrote the book. The same who has been a source of inspiration for my actions and thoughts for over thirty-five years. A simple, relatively unknown English philosopher who died at 48 years-old."

"But Jim. This stuff? I mean, I believe someone very wise wrote it. But someone had to get it to you at the Post Office. It wasn't really mailed in 1911," she said, but unsure of herself.

"The letter was post marked 1911. And I wrote it."

Jeanne didn't need to tell me she was confused. Her quiet body-language told me all I needed to know.

"Just believe what you believe," I said. "Feel what you read. Don't be concerned for all this ghost-writer details. Decide what is valuable. In the end, that is all which really matters."

Jeanne took the stack of papers and slipped them back inside the box from the three inch wide end we had carefully opened with a razor knife. She tried to push them all the way inside but seemed to be hitting something. She pulled the stack of papers back out and felt inside the empty box. She pulled from it a long yellow envelope, the sturdy kind with a string ties that couriers for accountants and business owners long ago used to send important correspondence and banking papers.

I undid the string and open the envelope. From it fell a letter. I began to read:

Dear Mr. Pratt,

I am so deeply honored to have welcomed you into my world. And as children's books begin with their tales of fantasy and wonder with, 'once upon a time,' my world and yours have intersected at Lamp Hill Lane. The magical meditative days at my cottage, which you enjoyed, held the same power for me many years ago.

You shall find that a man once yearned to bless the world with his entire fortune, a fortune not made of precious metals or backed by British Pounds Sterling. No, it was rather a treasure of the mind. He had not the scientific knowledge the world now possesses regarding the wonderful brain locked within the human heart, just the rudimentary theory of proper thought supplying positive personal outcomes and circumstance.

I do hope you have enjoyed this short treatise and the basic precept it embodies which I refer to as 'Success Through Power Thinking.' "I offer you this manuscript for publication. In it the reader will find the key to unlock those powers, which a modern 21ˢᵗ Century world of turmoil, war, stress, and information-overload, desperately needs if it is to ever become ready for a true and lasting millennial peace.

"I would be honored if you would title this humble tome after my first book, yet include the entire aphorism which for one hundred years of regret I have longed to see on the covers of my work.

"I have faith a well known publisher may wish to combine the former treatise with the new. Appropriately it may then be titled, 'As a Man Thinketh, in His Heart.' Your name along with mine should grace the cover. Please forward a copy from the first printing to the address indicated.

Oh, by the way. Did you find Hampton of Devon? I believe you shall find it in what you call your "time machine." Happy reading!

Faithfully, your fellow writer and servant,

James Allen

Broad Park Ave
Ilfracombe, Devon England

At moments like this silence is the only way to invite truth, comprehension, and closure.

44
FINAL CHAPTERS

Jeanne didn't wait for my signal. After a few minutes of stunned silence, she got up and went to the desk. Before I could get there she had rummaged through every box, drawer, and had almost turned the antique piece of office furniture upside down.

"Honey? Let me show you something," I said, gently directing her. "Push here," I said, pointing to the inside wall of the stack of drawers situated to the left and on top of the desk table itself.

"But…" she began in protest.

"Trust me," I interjected.

I stood back and she gave the wall a shove. It gave about three inches and she heard a 'click' indicating the catch for the false hiding panel had caught.

"Why didn't you tell me about this?" she asked.

"A man needs a few secrets. I guess the previous owner did as well."

She didn't reply. Both of us just stood there wondering if we were crazy, but with child-like anticipation all the same. It was as if a parent or guardian was giving us a treasure map, placing us on a hunt, and then allowing the joy of discovery to be our little secret.

"Go ahead," I prompted.

"What if there are spiders in there?" she returned. "I don't like spiders."

"There are no spiders," I whispered. "Only surprises."

"I'm not sticking my hand in there until you do first."

I raised my eyebrows in a question, and then proceeded. I positioned my bulk over the top of the desk to adequately reach and move my arm around inside the rectangular space twelve inches in length by twenty-four deep with about three inches diameter, give or take a quarter inch.

I couldn't reach the bottom of the space, and in fact had never needed to. I could always place something in there that I could grab from the top edge.

"Here, let me," Jeanne, with the slender arms, demanded. "Get out of my way."

I laughed, and of course was thrilled that she was becoming at least the believer, if not the delusional dreamer, I was. It was a nice feeling to have someone involved in this author fantasy that had begun over one year earlier with a search for the elusive author of a partially finished English love story.

She soon had her entire arm extended down into the panel. The stack of drawers was the type that set upon the desk but also extended to the floor in one seamless but bulky connected piece. I never imagined another hidden space inside, just the area I had found located at the desk top level.

"Well?" I asked. A smile creased her lips as she seemed to have grasped something. Gently coaxing it from its hiding place, she withdrew her arm to reveal a well used and dusty manila size envelope.

She laid it upon the desk top. "Your turn," she said, pleased with her discovery.

"WOW! I'm dreaming. Am I dreaming, Jeanne?"

"Just open it," she kindly scolded.

My palms were sweaty. My hands actually shook as I tried to untie the string that closed the flap to the aged envelope. With so much happening, and so fast, my mind almost couldn't determine fantasy from fact anymore. "I can't," I finally said. "You do it."

Jeanne took over. Delicate and capable fingers finally untied the secured flap. My heart raced to somewhat a sprinter's beat. I anticipated what James Allen's note promised of course, but still could hardly believe this much magic was available to us in so little time.

She pulled at the papers inside. I held my breath. The papers removed were covered in some sort of fine semi-transparent gift wrapping with a waxed feel, as if to protect them from the elements.

"So here it is," I breathed, as Jeanne set the stack upon the desk top.

We both stood there in awe. "Should I take the wrapping off?" she asked.

I almost said, "No." I wanted to savor this. These joys of child proportions don't often repeat themselves into adulthood. I had worked my entire life to employ the secrets of James Allen's multi-million selling tome of self-improvement and suddenly I was partnering with him.

The gap between time "past and present" had closed. He was here at the desk placing his beloved work inside the panel. I was here at the same desk removing it.

"Jim," Jeanne said, breaking me from my reverie. "I can't wait. Please?"

I obeyed and began to unwrap the translucent paper from what I knew I would find. I wished that this moment of discovery could last. I knew there was also a mission for these final chapters to a missing manuscript. The writer was offering a gift from beyond nine decades past. I pulled the stack of handwritten pages from the elegant wrapping. "*Hampton of Devon*," I whispered. "Welcome home."

45
RETURN TO ILFRACOMBE

It was early morning. I couldn't sleep. I walked down to the harbor before sunrise and thought about Jim Hyde and Miriam. I wondered if I should walk down the few blocks to Singh's bicycle shop, and the rare book store too, just to see what occupied those places.

I would be doing my official US book tour with a "kick-off" at The Bookery, back home in Lexington, in one week.*

The books would be delivered to stores nationwide the same week and then worldwide in three weeks following. My publisher wanted to do one spectacular publicity "kick off" of my book tours by sending me back here. This was a rare opportunity; taking advantage of last year's international "hoopla" over the "American Author Lost at Sea" story the BBC had reported, and that CNN and other television news networks back home had picked up on. No doubt they would all do a follow up story now that a book resulted. The BBC reporter who broke the story last year promised to meet me here and do a thorough study on how this book came to be.

If publicity ever was going to be a factor in selling a book in the United Kingdom, now was the time to get it started. Besides I had promised Jeanne this trip and I really needed to come back here, where it all began, and where it should conclude.

I was able to secure advance copies and brought some with me to Ilfracombe. Constable White would receive a copy, the staff at The Bath House Hotel as well. Media outlets, and several bookstores would receive their copy, along with 1,000 copies for the anticipated turnout to two nights of booked speeches here in town.

The truth would be told to the reporter today. It was up to her to believe what she would, but I felt certain she would retell it for public consumption in a way that would make it "stranger than fiction." And yet I felt any public judgment about my mental state would be redeemed by the coming forth of this book which I base upon the philosopher hometown hero, James Allen who died in 1912. Part of the untold story would be about the man's personality, his simple life, his several treatments on the power of thought upon character and circumstance, and now of that element most important above all, the "heart-mind alliance" for "power thinking."

Perhaps it all was just a dream. I still couldn't account for the loss of two weeks during the one I recall being here. These things were on my mind as I walked back toward the hotel.

I felt inside my trouser pocket for the medallion. It was there. I was sure that it had everything to do with the making of this book and yet I couldn't really explain it. I did find it on the ground at the gate to Lamp Hill where I had lost it in the brush on my first visit. And so it would return with me, along with a copy of the book I would be leaving upon the tumble-down walls of broken brick and stone cottage.

I turned one last time toward the sea before entering the hotel. The rising sun now caused a shimmering upon the water to the west that I knew would disappear as it crested on the eastern horizon. For a moment I thought I saw a small skiff with a young man and woman rowing back toward the quay…

"Naw!"

"Hi honey," I said as I entered our room.

No response.

"You okay, Jeanne?" I gently probed, not wanting to wake her from a deep jet-lag induced rest but eager to get this day going.

She yawned. "This is going to be a great day. I just know it. Just you and me… and no pressure."

"No pressure," I answered, feeling it actually begin to build.

She arose, began to ready herself and I contemplated the history of this room. I had asked for 205 when I booked the hotel. I pulled out my journal and noted my impressions regarding my return here. Just a few lines so far. I was determined to jot down every single thing out of the "norm" – should anything not considered "normal" occur.

What is normal, anyway? I posed in silence.

My normal isn't that of a person who "clocks in" to a job for 40 hours per week for twenty-five years. My normal is a certain serendipity of spirit and filtering accompanying experiences through the lens of a heart-minded process I had learned from a master; the godfather of the modern day inspirational self-improvement movement.

While my journey to Ilfracombe seems to have begun with the *Hampton of Devon* search, it really began with the book my mother gave me over thirty years earlier. Without it, and the influence of such a small but powerful fifty pages I would not ever have begun the journey in the first place.

I pondered upon that now; the patience that the Universe and God has for our lives – the timing of events and like a plant needing to grow, the right time for the fruit to ripen and be picked.

The famous one hundred year-old opus, *As a Man Thinketh,* came to me for my 19th birthday. I held that copy in my hands now. I scanned Mom's penned words she had transcribed into the title page: I didn't need to read her handwriting. I had memorized this truth long ago, in 1972.*

Mind is the master power that molds and makes and man is mind and ever more he takes, the tool of thought and shaping what he wills, brings forth a thousand joys, a thousand ills. He thinks in secret and it comes to pass. Environment is but his looking glass.

In quiet contemplation, my secret thoughts offered a life reviewed in mere seconds. The moments of stumbling, along with the triumphs, whisked before me. And now I knew he was right. The evidence of circumstance was judge and jury; both my greatest joy and also the indictment of how thoughts had translated to who I was, where I was, and how I lived. *Thank you James*, I whispered.

"Ready Jim?" Jeanne asked, donning a sweater and cap to greet the cool Atlantic Ocean air.

"I'd go with you anywhere," I answered. "Come on. We have a delivery to make."

46
SPECIAL DELIVERY

For whatever reason, I couldn't bring myself to go directly to the tumble-down cottage of Lamp Hill Lane. I knew if I saw it as it was I would suffer the bitter disappointment and revisit thoughts of delusion in spite of all that had happened in the one year since coming here.

So we went to a pleasant restaurant on High Street where we enjoyed a hearty English breakfast as we planned the day. I asked Jeanne if I could take her everywhere I had been, all that I thought I had seen. She sweetly agreed.

After all, Jeanne was now quite invested in this Fantasyland journey. She had read the 1902 edition of the treasured book by the master philosopher from Illracombe. And, she had held his handwritten pages in her hand – both the manuscript which had formed the guts of the book I was to leave off at Lamp Hill in "offering" to my muse and a copy of the new book.

After breakfast we walked and talked. I showed her the bay where the mist swallowed the craft holding a smiling and happy Jim and a beaming Miriam, dressed in the quaint costumes of the early 1900's. We walked along the boardwalk to the empty shop which once held bicycles and over which hung a sign that read, 'Singh's Bicycle Shoppe.'

I used up as much time as I could, sharing with my wife the very spot where I stood transfixed attempting to explain to her by cellular phone what my eyes had witnessed; that dancing multi-colored Aurora Borealis also called the Northern Lights.

"Remember what I said?" I asked, with my arm around her waist as we gazed out to sea.

"You said that you would have to bring me here…next year. You promised it," she replied.

"So I did. And here we are."

"Are you going to take me back to Lamp Hill Lane?" she asked next.

"Guess it's time, huh?" I answered.

She nodded. I felt for the coin in my pocket. With the coin I was assured entry into Singh's world. I only hoped…

"Jim?" she gently probed. "You are far away right now. I think it is time to go. The sun is setting. We have a book-signing tonight at the museum."

"Right. Shall we take a taxi?" I asked rhetorically, holding out my arm as we wandered the couple of blocks back to the hotel and had one called.

"Hello sir? Where to?" the cabbie asked.

"You look familiar," I said, as Jeanne and I scooted into the back seat.

"You are the American author who went missing last year."

"You have a good memory."

"I was questioned by the police several times. I should have a good memory. Where to sir? Or should I not ask – just drive directly there?"

"Good man," I said with a pat on the shoulder and a twenty dollar bill.

In moments the cabbie pulled over to the overgrown dirt path I had been calling Lamp Hill Lane for the past year. "Mr. Pratt, sir. I can wait? You won't be long will you?"

"Well, a bit, but we do need to be back in town in two hours for a…"

"For the book event," he said, finishing my sentence. "My wife and I are going. In fact she is there now saving us a front row seat. I think I shall just stay put and wait here for you, sir. The entire town will be out, and we wouldn't want to lose our newest citizen. I'd have a bit of explaining on my hands," he said with a grin.

"And we wouldn't want that," I replied. "Would we, Mrs. Pratt?" I asked turning to Jeanne.

"No we would not," she reassured.

"Okay then. We will return shortly," I said to the pleasant cabbie, offering a wave as I followed Jeanne, already walking ahead of me in some sort of shared anticipation.

"Can't get in without this," I offered, holding the coin out to her as I caught up from behind.

"Jim, what is it you expect to find here?" she asked.

"*My way*," I answered smiling.

She chuckled, knowing I referred to a JFK Indian Sikh baggage handler who had taught me that lesson before I ever arrived to England last year. "Whatever happened to him?" she wondered aloud.

I shrugged my shoulders. I had already brushed it off as synchronistic coincidence of a highly charged spiritual nature. *Thoughts are things,* I mumbled.

"What?" Jeanne asked as we reached the gate.

"Thoughts of Singh," I answered.

"Well, now what? We hold out the medallion and wait for him to arrive?" Jeanne questioned. I noted the pure childish hope in her countenance that I was serious, and that she could indeed experience a meeting with the mysterious horse and buggy driving messenger.

"Actually we watch for a rabbit with a stop watch," I replied with a grin.

She jabbed me in the arm, and then we both laughed.

"Come on. I have the coin right here." I took it from my pocket and held it up for her to see.

"Do you think it is there?" she whispered as we walked up the hill.

"Do I think 'what' is there?" I replied in a whisper equal to hers.

"The cottage?"

"Yes. But no matter what we see with our eyes, let's just enjoy the hill, the surroundings and leave our gift upon the altar of stones that was once our writing partner's home."

She shuddered.

I smiled and pulled her tight as we approached the old walls of my sanctuary on Lamp Hill.

48
JOURNEY'S END

Every journey must have an ending. And I knew this one of fanciful dreams, and ghosts, and imaginings, and voices, would end now, here, upon Lamp Hill.

"Jeanne will you wait right here?" I asked. "I need to do something alone," I added.

She handed me the package with an original manuscript and a first edition hard cover copy of *As a Man Thinketh...In His Heart*. "Say hello for me," she giggled, and then put herself to studying the serenity of the green brush covered landscape bordering the broad expanse of the Atlantic. "Don't forget to come back," she called out in nervous laughter as I walked toward the tumble-down structure. "Going around back," I called in reply, holding up the package. "Wait right here."

I wanted to see the well, the oak tree of pleasant afternoon naps and dreams, and a garden that existed only in my mind. I stopped at the entrance to the worn-out ruins and turned to wave. She nodded and returned my wave.

I took a deep breath and entered the make-believe world where a desk once held treasures for me here in Devon, and then delivered them to me there – back home in Virginia. I ambled, stopping here and there, through halls and rooms which once existed. "It was so real," I mumbled to no one.

I wondered where to leave the package with the copy of *As a Man Thinketh, In His Heart*, with my name and that of James Allen's – an offering of sorts to the ghosts of Lamp Hill Lane.

From the inside of the ruins I noticed the sun setting far quicker than I had anticipated. With its sinking into the vast Atlantic sea the sky began to show colors I had enjoyed before. The dancing Aurora looked as if it might return and I was eager to share this with Jeanne. But first, the task at hand, and then we could go back into town, and before the book event wander along the harbor and enjoy the romance of the heavenly Northern waltz.

I knew Jeanne would be getting nervous and so I closed my eyes and tried to focus upon hearing or feeling something similar to my fanciful days spent here, but missing to the rest of the world. I imagined being in the pleasant bed and breakfast with the Indian caretaker and home grown foods, and simple living, and no sounds but nature, and no cares but reading text written in long-hand, and good books of authors long departed from the world, and...

The coin, I heard my mind speak softly. I reached into my pocket and held it tightly in my hand. "Nothing comes from nothing," I read, "In the process of time" I continued, "By heart" I finished as I flipped it over and over.

With a strange confidence that I could find the place to leave the book, I exited toward the back of the property. Sunset was rapidly giving way to total night-time splendor now.

I rubbed at my eyes as I tried to focus on the glistening ocean backdrop to the dancing curtain falling from the sky. Entranced, I walked toward the rainbow veil of light that seemed to draw up, as ACT I in a play does. It revealed a hunched-over man whistling a playful Irish tune, and working with a hoe at rows filled with lush green garden vegetables.

I froze still, not wanting this vision to lift and dissipate like so many had, but the warmth worked upon me and soon drew me closer to the apparition. *So real*, I whispered.

The gardener working neat rows for crops seemed to be waiting for someone. I felt eager to join who appeared to be a humble middle-aged man. Growing closer, not wishing to disturb the man, but wanting to know what the stranger knew of this place and its former residents, I finally mustered the courage to clear my throat.

The man, slight of stature, reddish full hair and beard and one who seemed ill-fitted to, and drowning in over-sized garden attire, simply turned to me and smiled, then offered me the sweetest words I had yet heard in all my time in England: "Welcome back to Lamp Hill Lane, *Master James.*"

49
REAL OR FANTASY

I concluded my visit in the garden and further promises were made. Real or fantasy? All I know is that the book I took found its owner, and home, and I was now floating on air back to Jeanne who I supposed was waiting rather impatiently for me out front.

It was dark except for the waning Northern Lights which had fully captivated Jeanne as I approached her.

"I'm back," I joyfully offered.

"Oh, Jim! Isn't it marvelous? Look," she said as her arm swept the panoramic play performed before her in the night sky.

I put my arms tightly around her and allowed her to enjoy the scene as I whispered, "It is marvelous! Mission accomplished."

"So magical," she replied, hardly noticing my comment.

"We'd better get going. Hope the cabbie is still there. We have that book event," I added. I was glad she had found some magic here, but secretly I wanted her to know what I knew, that this place had a soul and was two places. One place was a location of tumble-down proportions in the present moment of frantic schedules and misplaced values, and another one built by a man for his beloved wife and daughter, and cared for by his friend – a noble man of the East who possessed great virtue and honor.

As we slowly walked hand-in-hand down the hill, and with the ruins of the cottage visibly shrinking behind us, Jeanne finally took her eyes from the dazzling display above and asked, "Did you find what you were looking for?"

This was the moment of truth. I stopped her and asked her to look toward the top of the hill. "What do you see?"

"Old walls. Stones, and brick."

"You just asked me if I found what I was looking for. Now let me ask you, 'Did you?'"

"Partly. I now believe you weren't imagining things when you told me about your calls being interfered with by the Northern Lights, and how beautiful they were. It is a magical setting and I know you were inspired by this place to write what you did." Jeanne seemed to want to continue but hesitated.

"But?" I asked.

"I also wanted to see what you said was here. I was hoping for… Hoping that… I wanted to see…" she didn't finish.

She didn't have to. I knew she wished she could see what my imaginings had painted inside her mind. It was becoming real and part of her. And with all the unexplainable happenings back home; the desk revealing its secrets of a manuscript titled *Hampton of Devon*, the 1902 autographed copy of *As a Man Thinketh*, and now this quiet moment on a ghostly setting with a magical curtain drawn across it; she was ready, and I didn't have to be all alone with my secrets.

"I want you to close your eyes and let me guide you to the property boundaries where Singh left me off. Hold this," I said, handing Jeanne the medallion I had kept firmly in my grip. Once at the gate I turned both of us around. Jeanne giggled like a little girl being guided on a hunt for a hidden treasure.

"Keep your eyes closed," I counseled, as we reached the starting spot; the gate. "Now walk back towards the cottage with me. Open your heart Jeanne, and just walk forward."

"What are we doing?" she quizzed quietly as if not to interrupt the spirit of the secret hunt.

"You cannot open your eyes until you promise me that *your heart is open*. Once you feel that way, then slowly open your eyes."

We walked further. Jeanne finally physically relaxed as I held her hand in mine. "Your heart," I whispered. I fixed my gaze on her eyes as they slowly opened. "Describe what you are seeing," I tenderly commanded.

"Oh… Jim! It can't be… Jim?" she tearfully and excitedly cried. "How?" she forced, gasping at the vision of a beautifully lighted and silhouetted cottage on a hill disappearing with the final evaporation of dancing heavenly lights for a back drop.

I didn't need to say anything. We were feeling what our eyes could no longer hide in the clouded visions of human disbelief. I took the medallion and whispered the Latin inscribed in the center of the coin on either side: "*Ex Animo…*" I said.

⁊•⫷

We left Ilfracombe the next day after another book signing and speaking event to an overflow audience, but not before a final light show. The Northern Lights, just as they had entertained the night before, appeared to dazzle with their celestial dance; a ballet of movement and color that left one knowing God was the artist, and we the characters on a canvas of life filled with as much imagination as our hearts would allow.

After all, does it matter what really happened or why I came here in the first place? If what appeared to me and then to Jeanne is not ever seen by another, does it make it any less real? Perhaps what is more important is that message prophets long ago spoke of which guided truly wise ones in a better way to live. They were also the words a gentle philosopher of Lamp Hill Lane taught me; first on my nineteenth birthday and now as a ghostwriter of *our* book…

"As a man thinketh…in his heart, so is he."

EPILOGUE

To Fantasyland and Power Thinking

Jeanne is sleeping. Her right hand gently holds my left. My right hand makes this entry in my journal. I wish to jot my awareness of this drama filled with discovery, just as I would if I were a director saying, "that's a wrap," to a well-scripted screenplay.

I am not sure how much I scripted in advance unawares. By that I mean how much was written in my thoughts, and ultimately my heart before hand which caused my life to collide in a seeming synchronistic way with so many of Mr. Allen's century-old truth's.

Perhaps, I have thought, his truth's need retelling in order to attract a newer audience, one filled with so much sophistication and suffering from attention deficit, and perhaps that retelling is simply offering what I have experienced here. *Perhaps…*

I gazed over to my slumbering wife and marveled at how we had survived thirty years of ups and downs, losses and reversals, health and near death, and yet seemed to become more child-like with each other as a result. We had seen a lot of changes in over fifty years of living, rotary dial telephone service to the speed-of-light communications we now enjoy. But the one change we needed most was a return to the wonder years of innocent belief and child-like joy.

Along with my AARP Discount Card, I count these years of newly minted "senior citizenship" status as well earned, and wondrous.

Our return trip home would not take us through Dulles International in Virginia but Orlando, Florida. Just as the story had started out with Jeanne going to Disneyland on the west coast, I promised to enjoy her kind of fun, enduring the lines, and take time out for fantasyland on the east coast. We would soon be landing and then forget our cares as a couple of big kids at Disney World.

I don't like to admit it to Jeanne, but I like Fantasyland. Why is that? Is it the little boy in me? Or is it the Peter Pan possibilities of actually living in Neverland; of living free of worldly adult sophistries encumbering the soul – of never really growing up?

My friend Mark Kastleman and his wife LaDawn have been bitten by the same bug. So has film manager in L.A., Maryann Ridini-Spencer. A film production partner, Mary Jean Bentley and her athletic husband Kevin have surrendered to this same voice calling them to simple love and living. A publishing associate, Carlos Packard and his wife Keri, are starting to enjoy the freedom these ideas give as they parent a handful of children; they too wish the purity of child-like joy to be mingled with that which their own children naturally know.

I believe we all secretly possess a desire to return to childhood virtues in such a way that the "real world" of pressures, and the illusionary pursuit of "success" with all the outward rewards and trappings, is left somewhere behind. Here in Mr. Disney's place, everyone pur-chases a ticket and leaves that adult world at the gate for a day.

In the beginning of this tale I sent Jeanne to Fantasyland with family in California while I enjoyed a serious writer's investigative journey across "the pond."

In the end, we both found a *return to innocence* and joy that exists in not our mental thoughts alone; no, but a place filled with potential for constant happiness in spite of what life throws at us. It is James Allen's "privileged place." It is located in our hearts, and goes with us. It is our real home, and we are welcome at all hours to enter the gate; "in the center," where we "will find our way."

"Honey," I quietly voiced to my sleepy companion of three decades. "Wake up. We are almost home."

SUPPLEMENTAL INFORMATION

AUTHOR AFTER WORD*

What is real, and what is not? I asked the same question to the reader in the "Author For-ward."

All I can say is the characters, Miriam, Jim Hyde, Singh, James Allen – all are as real to me as my wife Jeanne, and my friends Mark and LaDawn Kastleman are. All played a part in this story, and all live.

I promised the reader that they might know more of the "true" incidents that have been asterisked (*) and helped develop the story. I now keep that promise to you.

You will recall my statement about how, "Strange things, unusual things can happen in Cyberspace." I now offer some of those tidbits of real truth mixed with fancy that created this story.

You must be asking yourself some of these questions by now: Is *Hampton of Devon* going to come out in book form? Where can I learn more about the Ten Power Thinking Princi-ples? Is Mark Kastleman a trainer and does he provide some answers about Power Thinking?

For more information on this tale and these questions visit the following website and fol-low the links: www.powerthink.com. Click "SECRETS of *AS A MAN THINKETH*" on the homepage. Pleasant reading and remember, "Nothing comes from nothing!"

James Michael Pratt
Ilfracombe, England
April 2, 2008

As A Man Thinketh

By

James Allen

The 1902 Bestselling Classic

"Mind is the Master power that moulds and makes, And Man is Mind, and evermore he takes the tool of thought, and, shaping what he wills, brings forth a thousand joys, a thousand ills. He thinks in secret, and it comes to pass. Environment is but his looking-glass."

-James Allen, As a Man Thinketh

James Michael Pratt Introduction

Getting to know James Allen (1864-1912) has been one of the great joys of my life. Born in Leicester County, England in 1864 he died of a prolonged illness at his home at age 48 in Devon, on the southwest coast of England, in the seaside village of Ilfracombe. While little has been known of the personal life of the man for most of one hundred years, more has recently come to light thanks to curious researchers, and an Ilfracombe biographer, John Woodcock who created a small history of both James and Lily Allen for the Ilfracombe Museum.[1]

James Allen never sought the fame and notoriety which most writers do. He was a humble man who lived modestly, yet comfortably, at 33 Broad Park Avenue in Ilfracombe with his wife Lily and daughter Nora in a home which still stands. Lily Allen loved and supported the urgency which propelled James to create nineteen life-improving works over a ten year period, and a subscription based magazine called the Epoch. She felt the one which he thought the least of his books would become the greatest. She was right.

Indeed, James Allen can be credited as one of the forerunners to, and perhaps the mentor of, all Twentieth Century self-improvement, success, and motivation teachers. *As a Man Thinketh* is owned by millions and has helped people become better in every area of their lives for over one hundred years. Because of its "evergreen" message it continues to outlive and outsell virtually all modern and new age "how to" books for life improvement.

To give you an idea of James Allen's productivity over a short span of time I offer the following perspective: I have been a published author for ten years, working day and night, to frame messages I hope will entertain and bless others lives. I have modern conveniences of automatic computer editing, storing, printing, and instantaneous internet fact finding (the world's greatest libraries at my fingertips) to aid me in this pursuit. I will have published 10 works in ten years by the end of 2008. Mr. Allen had libraries and the available copies of books they might locally carry. He used ink blotter, paper, and possibly with the advent of typewriters, indulged in a manual keyboard with inked ribbon and carbon paper to get the writing work done. James Allen accomplished 19 published works of inspiration and self-improvement in a ten year period.

He created a worldwide audience in his day, though few seemed to be of his native land. His fans ranged from India to New Zealand; Australia to the US. Today, virtually every country carries copies of his works. His books have stood the test of time. Regardless of all the tools available to me, will mine? This speaks to the greatness of the man in terms of devotion, belief, and mission-oriented determination. His writings reveal that much about him, but also of his lofty frame of reference in terms of "how to live" abundantly, fully, with joy, love, and purpose.

In His Own Words:

"I looked around upon the world and saw that it was shadowed by sorrow and scorched by the fierce fires of suffering. And I looked for the cause. I looked around, but I could not find it. I looked in books, but I could not find it. I looked within, and found there both the cause and the self-made nature of that cause. I looked again, and deeper, and found the remedy. I found one Law, the Law of Love; one Life, the life of adjustment to that Law; one Truth, the Truth of a conquered mind and a quiet and obedient heart.

"And I dreamed of writing books which would help men and women, whether rich or poor, learned or unlearned, worldly or unworldly to find within themselves the source of all success, all happiness, accomplishment, all truth. And the dream remained with me, and at last became substantial; and now I send forth these books into the world on a mission of healing and blessedness, knowing that they cannot fail to reach the homes and hearts of those who are waiting and ready to receive them." —James Allen

James Allen's influences included contemporaries such as Robert Emerson, Henry Drummond, Longfellow, Oliver Wendell Holmes, Mahatma Gandhi, Jacob Boehme, among others. The play writes and philosophers such as England's own Shakespeare, along with ancient Aristotle and Plato, further stimulated Allen to thought on deep matters of human nature.

James Allen was a believer in Christ but also in Buddha. He felt the church he had been born in to was empty and hollow and so did not associate with organized religion, but did not condemn those who did. His life was about greater faith in righteousness, and not less. In fact he called his fellow thinkers, "The Brotherhood of Righteousness."

His friendship's were of a diverse array of thinkers; artists, the religious, philosophical. He would meet once a week with these "power thinkers" to explore the human condition and seek answers to life mysteries. His retirement in Ilfracombe was pleasant where he indulged himself with pre-dawn retreats to a nearby hilltop called "The Cairn" to meditate. Daily gardening was also a therapeutic outlet for him. He suffered from an internal ailment and frailty which ultimately would weaken him and cause his early death.

A man of contemplation, James focused upon the inner man. This same "inside out" approach to life changing is preached today by such luminaries of the self-improvement world as Stephen Covey and Wayne Dyer, among others.

His writings reveal a spiritual man, yet eclectic as far as religious systems go. He could as easily use Judeo-Christian teachings or Far Eastern Yogic, Hindu, Taoism, Buddhist thought to produce the same results. In other words, the building of character to determine the quality of life one lives depends upon a principle based belief system, and most religious systems merge at intersections of belief regarding moral conduct and "right thinking" as James Allen would say. Just as many religions or spiritual systems are built upon similar principles of integrity, love, purpose, belief, and moral practices, so Allen found by exploring their roots he could come up with a system for wholesome living; both physically and spiritually.

I was first introduced to As a Man Thinketh by James Allen when my mother chose to give it to me for my 19th birthday. In my search for the "real James Allen" which took me to Ilfracombe, England, I was asked by a young American in London, Aaron Douglas of Texas, my purposes for traveling alone. I told him about my story and need to do an authentic and unscripted research in Mr. Allen's home town. Surprised he said, "My father gave me that book when I went to college and told me to read it over and over again." I felt validated by my new friend of a younger generation. A wise mother and father gave me a gift to help me develop "right thinking." It is gratifying to see this wisdom continued by the father of young Mr. Douglas.

I have been blessed every day since the first reading in April 1972. I believe the reader will be richly rewarded during this reading and I am delighted the publisher has chosen to offer this as a bonus book for your inspiration.

James M. Pratt
April 2, 2008
Ilfracombe Museum

1 James Allen 1864-1912, An Illustrated Biography, by John Woodcock 2003

Author's Foreword

This little volume (the result of meditation and experience) is not intended as an exhaustive treatise on the much-written-upon subject of the power of thought. It is suggestive rather than explanatory, its object being to stimulate men and women to the discovery and perception of the truth that—

"They themselves are makers of themselves."

by virtue of the thoughts, which they choose and encourage; that mind is the master-weaver, both of the inner garment of character and the outer garment of circumstance, and that, as they may have hitherto woven in ignorance and pain they may now weave in enlightenment and happiness.

James Allen 1902
Broad Park Avenue
Ilfracombe, England.

Sow a thought and you reap an action;
Sow an act and you reap a habit;
Sow a habit and you reap a character;
Sow a character and you reap a destiny.

— Ralph Waldo Emerson

Thought And Character

THE aphorism, "As a man thinketh in his heart so is he," not only embraces the whole of a man's being, but is so comprehensive as to reach out to every condition and circumstance of his life. A man is literally *what he thinks*, his character being the complete sum of all his thoughts.

As the plant springs from, and could not be without, the seed, so every act of a man springs from the hidden seeds of thought, and could not have appeared without them. This applies equally to those acts called "spontaneous" and "unpremeditated" as to those, which are deliberately executed.

Act is the blossom of thought, and joy and suffering are its fruits; thus does a man garner in the sweet and bitter fruitage of his own husbandry.

> *"Thought in the mind hath made us, What we are*
> *By thought was wrought and built. If a man's mind*
> *Hath evil thoughts, pain comes on him as comes*
> *The wheel the ox behind.... If one endure*
> *In purity of thought, joy follows him*
> *As his own shadow — sure."*

Man is a growth by law, and not a creation by artifice, and cause and effect is as absolute and undeviating in the hidden realm of thought as in the world of visible and material things. A noble and Godlike character is not a thing of favour or chance, but is the natural result of continued effort in right thinking, the effect of long-cherished association with Godlike thoughts. An ignoble and bestial character, by the same process, is the result of the continued harbouring of grovelling thoughts.

Man is made or unmade by himself; in the armoury of thought he forges the weapons by which he destroys himself; he also fashions the tools with which he builds for himself heavenly mansions of joy and strength and peace. By the right choice and true application of thought, man ascends to the Divine Perfection; by the abuse and wrong application of thought, he descends below the level of the beast. Between these two extremes are all the grades of character, and man is their maker and master.

Of all the beautiful truths pertaining to the soul which have been restored and brought to light in this age, none is more gladdening or fruitful of divine promise and confidence than this — that man is the master of thought, the moulder of character, and the maker and shaper of condition, environment, and destiny.

As a being of Power, Intelligence, and Love, and the lord of his own thoughts, man holds the key to every situation, and contains within himself that transforming and regenerative agency by which he may make himself what he wills.

Man is always the master, even in his weaker and most abandoned state; but in his weakness and degradation he is the foolish master who misgoverns his "household." When he begins to reflect upon his condition, and to search diligently for the Law upon which his being is established, he then becomes the wise master, directing his energies with intelligence, and fashioning his thoughts to fruitful issues. Such is the *conscious* master, and man can only thus become by discovering *within himself* the laws of thought; which discovery is totally a matter of application, self analysis, and experience.

Only by much searching and mining, are gold and diamonds obtained, and man can find every truth connected with his being, if he will dig deep into the mine of his soul; and that he is the maker of his character, the moulder of his life, and the builder of his destiny, he may unerringly prove, if he will watch, control, and alter his thoughts, tracing their effects upon himself, upon others, and upon his life and circumstances, linking cause and effect by patient practice and investigation, and utilizing his every experience, even to the most trivial, everyday occurrence, as a means of obtaining that knowledge of himself which is Understanding, Wisdom, Power. In this direction, as in no other, is the law absolute that "He that seeketh findeth; and to him that knocketh it shall be opened;" for only by patience, practice, and ceaseless importunity can a man enter the Door of the Temple of Knowledge.

"A word is not a crystal, transparent and unchanged; it is the skin of a living thought, and may vary greatly in color and content according to the circumstances and the time in which it is used."
Oliver Wendell Holmes Jr.
American Associate Justice, Supreme Court

Effect Of Thought On Circumstances

MAN'S mind may be likened to a garden, which may be intelligently culti-vated or allowed to run wild; but whether cultivated or neglected, it must, and will, *bring forth*. If no useful seeds are *put* into it, then an abundance of useless weed-seeds will *fall* therein, and will continue to produce their kind.

Just as a gardener cultivates his plot, keeping it free from weeds, and grow-ing the flowers and fruits which he requires, so may a man tend the garden of his mind, weeding out all the wrong, useless, and impure thoughts, and cultivating toward perfection the flowers and fruits of right, useful, and pure thoughts. By pursuing this process, a man sooner or later discovers that he is the master-gar-dener of his soul, the director of his life. He also reveals, within himself, the laws of thought, and understands, with ever-increasing accuracy, how the thought-forces and mind elements operate in the shaping of his character, circumstances, and destiny.

Thought and character are one, and as character can only manifest and dis-cover itself through environment and circumstance, the outer conditions of a per-son's life will always be found to be harmoniously related to his inner state. This does not mean that a man's circumstances at any given time are an indication of his *entire* character, but that those circumstances are so intimately connected with some vital thought-element within himself that, for the time being, they are in-dispensable to his development.

Every man is where he is by the law of his being; the thoughts which he has built into his character have brought him there, and in the arrangement of his life there is no element of chance, but all is the result of a law which cannot err. This is just as true of those who feel "out of harmony" with their surroundings as of those who are contented with them.

As a progressive and evolving being, man is where he is that he may learn that he may grow; and as he learns the spiritual lesson which any circumstance con-tains for him, it passes away and gives place to other circumstances.

Man is buffeted by circumstances so long as he believes himself to be the crea-ture of outside conditions, but when he realizes that he is a creative power, and that he may command the hidden soil and seeds of his being out of which cir-cumstances grow, he then becomes the rightful master of himself.

That circumstances grow out of thought every man knows who has for any length of time practised self-control and self-purification, for he will have no-ticed that the alteration in his circumstances has been in exact ratio with his al-tered mental condition. So true is this that when a man earnestly applies himself to remedy the defects in his character, and makes swift and marked progress, he passes rapidly through a succession of vicissitudes.

The soul attracts that which it secretly harbours; that which it loves, and also that which it fears; it reaches the height of its cherished aspirations; it falls to the level of its unchastened desires, — and circumstances are the means by which the soul receives its own.

Every thought-seed sown or allowed to fall into the mind, and to take root there, produces its own, blossoming sooner or later into act, and bearing its own fruitage of opportunity and circumstance. Good thoughts bear good fruit, bad thoughts bad fruit.

The outer world of circumstance shapes itself to the inner world of thought, and both pleasant and unpleasant external conditions are factors, which make for the ultimate good of the individual. As the reaper of his own harvest, man learns both by suffering and bliss.

Following the inmost desires, aspirations, thoughts, by which he allows himself to be dominated, (pursuing the will-o'-the-wisps of impure imaginings or steadfastly walking the highway of strong and high endeavour), a man at last arrives at their fruition and fulfilment in the outer conditions of his life. The laws of growth and adjustment everywhere obtain.

A man does not come to the almshouse or the jail by the tyranny of fate or circumstance, but by the pathway of grovelling thoughts and base desires. Nor does a pure-minded man fall suddenly into crime by stress of any mere external force; the criminal thought had long been secretly fostered in the heart, and the hour of opportunity revealed its gathered power. Circumstance does not make the man; it reveals him to himself No such conditions can exist as descending into vice and its attendant sufferings apart from vicious inclinations, or ascending into virtue and its pure happiness without the continued cultivation of virtuous aspirations; and man, therefore, as the lord and master of thought, is the maker of himself the shaper and author of environment. Even at birth the soul comes to its own and through every step of its earthly pilgrimage it attracts those combinations of conditions which reveal itself, which are the reflections of its own purity and, impurity, its strength and weakness.

Men do not attract that which they *want*, but that which they *are*. Their whims, fancies, and ambitions are thwarted at every step, but their inmost thoughts and desires are fed with their own food, be it foul or clean. The "divinity that shapes our ends" is in ourselves; it is our very self. Only himself manacles man: thought and action are the gaolers of Fate — they imprison, being base; they are also the angels of Freedom — they liberate, being noble. Not what he wishes and prays for does a man get, but what he justly earns. His wishes and prayers are only gratified and answered when they harmonize with his thoughts and actions.

In the light of this truth, what, then, is the meaning of "fighting against circumstances?" It means that a man is continually revolting against an *effect* without, while all the time he is nourishing and preserving its *cause* in his heart. That cause may take the form of a conscious vice or an unconscious weakness; but whatever it is, it stubbornly retards the efforts of its possessor, and thus calls aloud for remedy.

Men are anxious to improve their circumstances, but are unwilling to improve themselves; they therefore remain bound. The man who does not shrink from self-crucifixion can never fail to accomplish the object upon which his heart is set. This is as true of earthly as of heavenly things. Even the man whose sole object is to acquire wealth must be prepared to make great personal sacrifices before he can accomplish his object; and how much more so he who would realize a strong and well-poised life?

Here is a man who is wretchedly poor. He is extremely anxious that his surroundings and home comforts should be improved, yet all the time he shirks his work, and considers he is justified in trying to deceive his employer on the ground of the insufficiency of his wages. Such a man does not understand the simplest rudiments of those principles which are the basis of true prosperity, and is not only totally unfitted to rise out of his wretchedness, but is actually attracting to himself a still deeper wretchedness by dwelling in, and acting out, indolent, deceptive, and unmanly thoughts.

Here is a rich man who is the victim of a painful and persistent disease as the result of gluttony. He is willing to give large sums of money to get rid of it, but he will not sacrifice his gluttonous desires. He wants to gratify his taste for rich and unnatural viands and have his health as well. Such a man is totally unfit to have health, because he has not yet learned the first principles of a healthy life.

Here is an employer of labour who adopts crooked measures to avoid paying the regulation wage, and, in the hope of making larger profits, reduces the wages of his workpeople. Such a man is altogether unfitted for prosperity, and when he finds himself bankrupt, both as regards reputation and riches, he blames circumstances, not knowing that he is the sole author of his condition.

I have introduced these three cases merely as illustrative of the truth that man is the causer (though nearly always is unconsciously) of his circumstances, and that, whilst aiming at a good end, he is continually frustrating its accomplishment by encouraging thoughts and desires which cannot possibly harmonize with that end. Such cases could be multiplied and varied almost indefinitely, but this is not necessary, as the reader can, if he so resolves, trace the action of the laws of thought in his own mind and life, and until this is done, mere external facts cannot serve as a ground of reasoning.

Circumstances, however, are so complicated, thought is so deeply rooted, and the conditions of happiness vary so, vastly with individuals, that a man's entire soul-condition (although it may be known to himself) cannot be judged by another from the external aspect of his life alone. A man may be honest in certain directions, yet suffer privations; a man may be dishonest in certain directions, yet acquire wealth; but the conclusion usually formed that the one man fails *because of his particular honesty,* and that the other *prospers because of his particular dishonesty,* is the result of a superficial judgment, which assumes that the dishonest man is almost totally corrupt, and the honest man almost entirely virtuous. In the light of a deeper knowledge and wider experience such judgment is found to be erroneous. The dishonest man may have some admirable virtues, which the other does, not possess; and the honest man obnoxious vices which are absent in the other. The honest man reaps the good results of his honest thoughts and acts; he also brings upon himself the sufferings, which his vices produce. The dishonest man likewise garners his own suffering and happiness.

It is pleasing to human vanity to believe that one suffers because of one's virtue; but not until a man has extirpated every sickly, bitter, and impure thought from his mind, and washed every sinful stain from his soul, can he be in a position to know and declare that his sufferings are the result of his good, and not of his bad qualities; and on the way to, yet long before he has reached, that supreme perfection, he will have found, working in his mind and life, the Great Law which is absolutely just, and which cannot, therefore, give good for evil, evil for good. Possessed of such knowledge, he will then know, looking back upon his past ignorance and blindness, that his life is, and always was, justly ordered, and that all his past experiences, good and bad, were the equitable outworking of his evolving, yet unevolved self.

Good thoughts and actions can never produce bad results; bad thoughts and actions can never produce good results. This is but saying that nothing can come from corn but corn, nothing from nettles but nettles. Men understand this law in the natural world, and work with it; but few understand it in the mental and moral world (though its operation there is just as simple and undeviating), and they, therefore, do not co-operate with it.

Suffering is *always* the effect of wrong thought in some direction. It is an indication that the individual is out of harmony with himself, with the Law of his being. The sole and supreme use of suffering is to purify, to burn out all that is useless and impure. Suffering ceases for him who is pure. There could be no object in burning gold after the dross had been removed, and a perfectly pure and enlightened being could not suffer.

The circumstances, which a man encounters with suffering, are the result of his own mental in harmony. The circumstances, which a man encounters with blessedness, are the result of his own mental harmony. Blessedness, not material possessions, is the measure of right thought; wretchedness, not lack of material possessions, is the measure of wrong thought. A man may be cursed and rich; he may be blessed and poor. Blessedness and riches are only joined together when the riches are rightly and wisely used; and the poor man only descends into wretchedness when he regards his lot as a burden unjustly imposed.

Indigence and indulgence are the two extremes of wretchedness. They are both equally unnatural and the result of mental disorder. A man is not rightly conditioned until he is a happy, healthy, and prosperous being; and happiness, health, and prosperity are the result of a harmonious adjustment of the inner with the outer, of the man with his surroundings.

A man only begins to be a man when he ceases to whine and revile, and commences to search for the hidden justice which regulates his life. And as he adapts his mind to that regulating factor, he ceases to accuse others as the cause of his condition, and builds himself up in strong and noble thoughts; ceases to kick against circumstances, but begins to *use* them as aids to his more rapid progress, and as a means of discovering the hidden powers and possibilities within himself.

Law, not confusion, is the dominating principle in the universe; justice, not injustice, is the soul and substance of life; and righteousness, not corruption, is the moulding and moving force in the spiritual government of the world. This being so, man has but to right himself to find that the universe is right; and during the process of putting himself right he will find that as he alters his thoughts towards things and other people, things and other people will alter towards him.

The proof of this truth is in every person, and it therefore admits of easy investigation by systematic introspection and self-analysis. Let a man radically alter his thoughts, and he will be astonished at the rapid transformation it will effect in the material conditions of his life. Men imagine that thought can be kept secret, but it cannot; it rapidly crystallizes into habit, and habit solidifies into circumstance. Bestial thoughts crystallize into habits of drunkenness and sensuality, which solidify into circumstances of destitution and disease: impure thoughts of every kind crystallize into enervating and confusing habits, which solidify into distracting and adverse circumstances: thoughts of fear, doubt, and indecision crystallize into weak, unmanly, and irresolute habits, which solidify into circumstances of failure, indigence, and slavish dependence: lazy thoughts crystallize into habits of uncleanliness and dishonesty, which solidify into circumstances of foulness and beggary: hateful and condemnatory thoughts crystallize into habits of accusation and violence, which solidify into circumstances of injury and persecution: selfish thoughts of all kinds crystallize into habits of self-seeking, which solidify into circumstances more or less distressing. On the other hand, beautiful thoughts of all kinds crystallize into habits of grace and kindliness, which solidify into genial and sunny circumstances: pure thoughts crystallize into habits of temperance and self-control, which solidify into circumstances of repose and peace: thoughts of courage, self-reliance, and decision crystallize into manly habits, which solidify into circumstances of success, plenty, and freedom: energetic thoughts crystallize into habits of cleanliness and industry, which solidify into circumstances of pleasantness: gentle and forgiving thoughts crystallize into habits of gentleness, which solidify into protective and preservative circumstances: loving and unselfish thoughts crystallize into habits of self-forgetfulness for others, which solidify into circumstances of sure and abiding prosperity and true riches.

A particular train of thought persisted in, be it good or bad, cannot fail to produce its results on the character and circumstances. A man cannot *directly* choose his circumstances, but he can choose his thoughts, and so indirectly, yet surely, shape his circumstances.

Nature helps every man to the gratification of the thoughts, which he most encourages, and opportunities are presented which will most speedily bring to the surface both the good and evil thoughts.

Let a man cease from his sinful thoughts, and all the world will soften towards him, and be ready to help him; let him put away his weakly and sickly thoughts, and lo, opportunities will spring up on every hand to aid his strong resolves; let him encourage good thoughts, and no hard fate shall bind him down to wretchedness and shame. The world is your kaleidoscope, and the varying combinations of colours, which at every succeeding moment it presents to you are the exquisitely adjusted pictures of your ever-moving thoughts.

"You will be what you will to be;
Let failure find its false content
In that poor word, 'environment,'
But spirit scorns it, and is free.
"It masters time, it conquers space;
It cowes that boastful trickster, Chance,
And bids the tyrant Circumstance
Uncrown, and fill a servant's place.
"The human Will, that force unseen,
The offspring of a deathless Soul,
Can hew a way to any goal,
Though walls of granite intervene.
"Be not impatient in delays
But wait as one who understands;
When spirit rises and commands
The gods are ready to obey."

Effect Of Thought
On Health And The Body

THE body is the servant of the mind. It obeys the operations of the mind, whether they be deliberately chosen or automatically expressed. At the bidding of unlawful thoughts the body sinks rapidly into disease and decay; at the command of glad and beautiful thoughts it becomes clothed with youthfulness and beauty.

Disease and health, like circumstances, are rooted in thought. Sickly thoughts will express themselves through a sickly body. Thoughts of fear have been known to kill a man as speedily as a bullet, and they are continually killing thousands of people just as surely though less rapidly. The people who live in fear of disease are the people who get it. Anxiety quickly demoralizes the whole body, and lays it open to the, entrance of disease; while impure thoughts, even if not physically indulged, will soon shatter the nervous system.

Strong, pure, and happy thoughts build up the body in vigour and grace. The body is a delicate and plastic instrument, which responds readily to the thoughts by which it is impressed, and habits of thought will produce their own effects, good or bad, upon it.

Men will continue to have impure and poisoned blood, so long as they propagate unclean thoughts. Out of a clean heart comes a clean life and a clean body. Out of a defiled mind proceeds a defiled life and a corrupt body. Thought is the fount of action, life, and manifestation; make the fountain pure, and all will be pure.

Change of diet will not help a man who will not change his thoughts. When a man makes his thoughts pure, he no longer desires impure food.

Clean thoughts make clean habits. The so-called saint who does not wash his body is not a saint. He who has strengthened and purified his thoughts does not need to consider the malevolent microbe.

If you would protect your body, guard your mind. If you would renew your body, beautify your mind. Thoughts of malice, envy, disappointment, despondency, rob the body of its health and grace. A sour face does not come by chance; it is made by sour thoughts. Wrinkles that mar are drawn by folly, passion, and pride.

I know a woman of ninety-six who has the bright, innocent face of a girl. I know a man well under middle age whose face is drawn into inharmonious contours. The one is the result of a sweet and sunny disposition; the other is the outcome of passion and discontent.

As you cannot have a sweet and wholesome abode unless you admit the air and sunshine freely into your rooms, so a strong body and a bright, happy, or serene countenance can only result from the free admittance into the mind of thoughts of joy and goodwill and serenity.

On the faces of the aged there are wrinkles made by sympathy, others by strong and pure thought, and others are carved by passion: who cannot distinguish them? With those who have lived righteously, age is calm, peaceful, and softly mellowed, like the setting sun. I have recently seen a philosopher on his deathbed. He was not old except in years. He died as sweetly and peacefully as he had lived.

There is no physician like cheerful thought for dissipating the ills of the body; there is no comforter to compare with goodwill for dispersing the shadows of grief and sorrow. To live continually in thoughts of ill will, cynicism, suspicion, and envy, is to be confined in a self made prison-hole. But to think well of all, to be cheerful with all, to patiently learn to find the good in all — such unselfish thoughts are the very portals of heaven; and to dwell day by day in thoughts of peace toward every creature will bring abounding peace to their possessor.

Thought And Purpose

Until thought is linked with purpose there is no intelligent accomplishment. With the majority the bark of thought is allowed to "drift" upon the ocean of life. Aimlessness is a vice, and such drifting must not continue for him who would steer clear of catastrophe and destruction.

They who have no central purpose in their life fall an easy prey to petty worries, fears, troubles, and self-pityings, all of which are indications of weakness, which lead, just as surely as deliberately planned sins (though by a different route), to failure, unhappiness, and loss, for weakness cannot persist in a power evolving universe.

A man should conceive of a legitimate purpose in his heart, and set out to accomplish it. He should make this purpose the centralizing point of his thoughts. It may take the form of a spiritual ideal, or it may be a worldly object, according to his nature at the time being; but whichever it is, he should steadily focus his thought-forces upon the object, which he has set before him. He should make this purpose his supreme duty, and should devote himself to its attainment, not allowing his thoughts to wander away into ephemeral fancies, longings, and imaginings. This is the royal road to self-control and true concentration of thought. Even if he fails again and again to accomplish his purpose (as he necessarily must until weakness is overcome), the *strength of character gained* will be the measure of *his true* success, and this will form a new starting-point for future power and triumph.

Those who are not prepared for the apprehension of a *great* purpose should fix the thoughts upon the faultless performance of their duty, no matter how insignificant their task may appear. Only in this way can the thoughts be gathered and focussed, and resolution and energy be developed, which being done, there is nothing which may not be accomplished.

The weakest soul, knowing its own weakness, and believing this truth *that strength can only be developed by effort and practice,* will, thus believing, at once begin to exert itself, and, adding effort to effort, patience to patience, and strength to strength, will never cease to develop, and will at last grow divinely strong.

As the physically weak man can make himself strong by careful and patient training, so the man of weak thoughts can make them strong by exercising himself in right thinking.

To put away aimlessness and weakness, and to begin to think with purpose, is to enter the ranks of those strong ones who only recognize failure as one of the pathways to attainment; who make all conditions serve them, and who think strongly, attempt fearlessly, and accomplish masterfully.

Having conceived of his purpose, a man should mentally mark out a *straight* pathway to its achievement, looking neither to the right nor the left. Doubts and fears should be rigorously excluded; they are disintegrating elements, which break up the straight line of effort, rendering it crooked, ineffectual, useless. Thoughts of doubt and fear never accomplished anything, and never can. They always lead to failure. Purpose, energy, power to do, and all strong thoughts cease when doubt and fear creep in.

The will to do springs from the knowledge that we *can* do. Doubt and fear are the great enemies of knowledge, and he who encourages them, who does not slay them. thwarts himself at every step.

He who has conquered doubt and fear has conquered failure. His every, thought is allied with power, and all difficulties are bravely met and wisely over-come. His purposes are seasonably planted, and they bloom and bring forth fruit, which does not fall prematurely to the ground.

Thought allied fearlessly to purpose becomes creative force: he who *knows* this is ready to become something higher and stronger than a mere bundle of wavering thoughts and fluctuating sensations; he who *does* this has become the conscious and intelligent wielder of his mental powers.

The Thought-Factor In Achievement

ALL that a man achieves and all that he fails to achieve is the direct result of his own thoughts. In a justly ordered universe, where loss of equipoise would mean total destruction, individual responsibility must be absolute. A man's weakness and strength, purity and impurity, are his own, and not another man's; they are brought about by himself, and not by another; and they can only be altered by himself, never by another. His condition is also his own, and not another man's. His suffering and his happiness are evolved from within. As he thinks, so he is; as he continues to think, so he remains.

A strong man cannot help a weaker unless that weaker is *willing* to be helped, and even then the weak man must become strong of himself; he must, by his own efforts, develop the strength which he admires in another. None but himself can alter his condition.

It has been usual for men to think and to say, "Many men are slaves because one is an oppressor; let us hate the oppressor." Now, however, there is amongst an increasing few a tendency to reverse this judgment, and to say, "One man is an oppressor because many are slaves; let us despise the slaves."

The truth is that oppressor and slave are co-operators in ignorance, and, while seeming to afflict each other, are in reality afflicting themselves. A perfect Knowledge perceives the action of law in the weakness of the oppressed and the misapplied power of the oppressor; a perfect Love, seeing the suffering, which both states entail, condemns neither; a perfect Compassion embraces both oppressor and oppressed.

He who has conquered weakness, and has put away all selfish thoughts, belongs neither to oppressor nor oppressed. He is free.

A man can only rise, conquer, and achieve by lifting up his thoughts. He can only remain weak, and abject, and miserable by refusing to lift up his thoughts.

Before a man can achieve anything, even in worldly things, he must lift his thoughts above slavish animal indulgence. He may not, in order to succeed, give up all animality and selfishness, by any means; but a portion of it must, at least, be sacrificed. A man whose first thought is bestial indulgence could neither think clearly nor plan methodically; he could not find and develop his latent resources, and would fail in any undertaking. Not having commenced to manfully control his thoughts, he is not in a position to control affairs and to adopt serious responsibilities. He is not fit to act independently and stand alone. But he is limited only by the thoughts, which he chooses.

There can be no progress, no achievement without sacrifice, and a man's worldly success will be in the measure that he sacrifices his confused animal thoughts, and fixes his mind on the development of his plans, and the strengthening of his resolution and self-reliance. And the higher he lifts his thoughts, the more manly, upright, and righteous he becomes, the greater will be his success, the more blessed and enduring will be his achievements.

The universe does not favour the greedy, the dishonest, the vicious, although on the mere surface it may sometimes appear to do so; it helps the honest, the magnanimous, the virtuous. All the great Teachers of the ages have declared this in varying forms, and to prove and know it a man has but to persist in making himself more and more virtuous by lifting up his thoughts.

Intellectual achievements are the result of thought consecrated to the search for knowledge, or for the beautiful and true in life and nature. Such achievements may be sometimes connected with vanity and ambition, but they are not the outcome of those characteristics; they are the natural outgrowth of long and arduous effort, and of pure and unselfish thoughts.

Spiritual achievements are the consummation of holy aspirations. He who lives constantly in the conception of noble and lofty thoughts, who dwells upon all that is pure and unselfish, will, as surely as the sun reaches its zenith and the moon its full, become wise and noble in character, and rise into a position of influence and blessedness.

Achievement, of whatever kind, is the crown of effort, the diadem of thought. By the aid of self-control, resolution, purity, righteousness, and well-directed thought a man ascends; by the aid of animality, indolence, impurity, corruption, and confusion of thought a man descends.

A man may rise to high success in the world, and even to lofty altitudes in the spiritual realm, and again descend into weakness and wretchedness by allowing arrogant, selfish, and corrupt thoughts to take possession of him.

Victories attained by right thought can only be maintained by watchfulness. Many give way when success is assured, and rapidly fall back into failure.

All achievements, whether in the business, intellectual, or spiritual world, are the result of definitely directed thought, are governed by the same law and are of the same method; the only difference lies in *the object of attainment*.

He who would accomplish little must sacrifice little; he who would achieve much must sacrifice much; he who would attain highly must sacrifice greatly.

Visions And Ideals

THE dreamers are the saviours of the world. As the visible world is sustained by the invisible, so men, through all their trials and sins and sordid vocations, are nourished by the beautiful visions of their solitary dreamers. Humanity cannot forget its dreamers; it cannot let their ideals fade and die; it lives in them; it knows them as they *realities* which it shall one day see and know.

Composer, sculptor, painter, poet, prophet, sage, these are the makers of the after-world, the architects of heaven. The world is beautiful because they have lived; without them, labouring humanity would perish.

He who cherishes a beautiful vision, a lofty ideal in his heart, will one day realize it. Columbus cherished a vision of another world, and he discovered it; Copernicus fostered the vision of a multiplicity of worlds and a wider universe, and he revealed it; Buddha beheld the vision of a spiritual world of stainless beauty and perfect peace, and he entered into it.

Cherish your visions; cherish your ideals; cherish the music that stirs in your heart, the beauty that forms in your mind, the loveliness that drapes your purest thoughts, for out of them will grow all delightful conditions, all, heavenly environment; of these, if you but remain true to them, your world will at last be built.

To desire is to obtain; to aspire is to, achieve. Shall man's basest desires receive the fullest measure of gratification, and his purest aspirations starve for lack of sustenance? Such is not the Law: such a condition of things can never obtain: "ask and receive."

Dream lofty dreams, and as you dream, so shall you become. Your Vision is the promise of what you shall one day be; your Ideal is the prophecy of what you shall at last unveil.

The greatest achievement was at first and for a time a dream. The oak sleeps in the acorn; the bird waits in the egg; and in the highest vision of the soul a waking angel stirs. Dreams are the seedlings of realities.

Your circumstances may be uncongenial, but they shall not long remain so if you but perceive an Ideal and strive to reach it. You cannot travel *within* and stand still *without.* Here is a youth hard pressed by poverty and labour; confined long hours in an unhealthy workshop; unschooled, and lacking all the arts of refinement. But he dreams of better things; he thinks of intelligence, of refinement, of grace and beauty. He conceives of, mentally builds up, an ideal condition of life; the vision of a wider liberty and a larger scope takes possession of him; unrest urges him to action, and he utilizes all his spare time and means, small though they are, to the development of his latent powers and resources. Very soon so altered has his mind become that the workshop can no longer hold him. It has become so out of harmony with his mentality that it falls out of his life as a garment is cast aside, and, with the growth of opportunities, which fit the scope of his expanding powers, he passes out of it forever. Years later we see this youth as a full-grown man. We find him a master of certain forces of the mind, which he wields with worldwide influence and almost unequalled power. In his hands he holds the cords of gigantic responsibilities; he speaks, and lo, lives are changed; men and women hang upon his words and remould their characters, and, sunlike, he becomes the fixed and luminous centre round which innumerable destinies revolve. He has realized the Vision of his youth. He has become one with his Ideal.

And you, too, youthful reader, will realize the Vision (not the idle wish) of your heart, be it base or beautiful, or a mixture of both, for you will always gravitate toward that which you, secretly, most love. Into your hands will be placed the exact results of your own thoughts; you will receive that which you earn; no more, no less. Whatever your present environment may be, you will fall, remain, or rise with your thoughts, your Vision, your Ideal. You will become as small as your controlling desire; as great as your dominant aspiration: in the beautiful words of Stanton Kirkham Davis, "You may be keeping accounts, and presently you shall walk out of the door that for so long has seemed to you the barrier of your ideals, and shall find yourself before an audience — the pen still behind your ear, the ink stains on your fingers and then and there shall pour out the torrent of your inspiration. You may be driving sheep, and you shall wander to the city-bucolic and open-mouthed; shall wander under the intrepid guidance of the spirit into the studio of the master, and after a time he shall say, 'I have nothing more to teach you.' And now you have become the master, who did so recently dream of great things while driving sheep. You shall lay down the saw and the plane to take upon yourself the regeneration of the world."

The thoughtless, the ignorant, and the indolent, seeing only the apparent effects of things and not the things themselves, talk of luck, of fortune, and chance. Seeing a man grow rich, they say, "How lucky he is!" Observing another become intellectual, they exclaim, "How highly favoured he is!" And noting the saintly character and wide influence of another, they remark, "How chance aids him at every turn!" They do not see the trials and failures and struggles which these men have voluntarily encountered in order to gain their experience; have no knowledge of the sacrifices they have made, of the undaunted efforts they have put forth, of the faith they have exercised, that they might overcome the apparently insurmountable, and realize the Vision of their heart. They do not know the darkness and the heartaches; they only see the light and joy, and call it "luck". They do not see the long and arduous journey, but only behold the pleasant goal, and call it "good fortune," do not understand the process, but only perceive the result, and call it chance.

In all human affairs there are *efforts*, and there are *results*, and the strength of the effort is the measure of the result. Chance is not. Gifts, powers, material, intellectual, and spiritual possessions are the fruits of effort; they are thoughts completed, objects accomplished, visions realized.

The Vision that you glorify in your mind, the Ideal that you enthrone in your heart — this you will build your life by, this you will become.

Serenity

CALMNESS of mind is one of the beautiful jewels of wisdom. It is the result of long and patient effort in self-control. Its presence is an indication of ripened experience, and of a more than ordinary knowledge of the laws and operations of thought.

A man becomes calm in the measure that he understands himself as a thought evolved being, for such knowledge necessitates the understanding of others as the result of thought, and as he develops a right understanding, and sees more and more clearly the internal relations of things by the action of cause and effect he ceases to fuss and fume and worry and grieve, and remains poised, steadfast, serene.

The calm man, having learned how to govern himself, knows how to adapt himself to others; and they, in turn, reverence his spiritual strength, and feel that they can learn of him and rely upon him. The more tranquil a man becomes, the greater is his success, his influence, his power for good. Even the ordinary trader will find his business prosperity increase as he develops a greater self-control and equanimity, for people will always prefer to deal with a man whose demeanour is strongly equable.

The strong, calm man is always loved and revered. He is like a shade-giving tree in a thirsty land, or a sheltering rock in a storm. "Who does not love a tranquil heart, a sweet-tempered, balanced life? It does not matter whether it rains or shines, or what changes come to those possessing these blessings, for they are always sweet, serene, and calm. That exquisite poise of character, which we call serenity is the last lesson of culture, the fruitage of the soul. It is precious as wisdom, more to be desired than gold — yea, than even fine gold. How insignificant mere money seeking looks in comparison with a serene life — a life that dwells in the ocean of Truth, beneath the waves, beyond the reach of tempests, in the Eternal Calm!

"How many people we know who sour their lives, who ruin all that is sweet and beautiful by explosive tempers, who destroy their poise of character, and make bad blood! It is a question whether the great majority of people do not ruin their lives and mar their happiness by lack of self-control. How few people we meet in life who are well balanced, who have that exquisite poise which is characteristic of the finished character!

Yes, humanity surges with uncontrolled passion, is tumultuous with ungoverned grief, is blown about by anxiety and doubt only the wise man, only he whose thoughts are controlled and purified, makes the winds and the storms of the soul obey him.

Tempest-tossed souls, wherever ye may be, under whatsoever conditions ye may live, know this in the ocean of life the isles of Blessedness are smiling, and the sunny shore of your ideal awaits your coming. Keep your hand firmly upon the helm of thought. In the bark of your soul reclines the commanding Master; He does but sleep: wake Him. Self-control is strength; Right Thought is mastery; Calmness is power. Say unto your heart, "Peace, be still!"

ABOUT THE AUTHOR

New York Times and USA Today bestselling author, James Michael Pratt is the author of nine published works, including soon-to-be CBS Hallmark Hall of Fame based upon his first international release, The Last Valentine. His family-friendly novels delving into the complexities of war, love and relationships, and history have earned him the accolades of critics. Booklist called him, "A master of moral fiction." Publisher's Weekly said of The Lighthouse Keeper, "His simple story will please the readers ready for a good cry." His novels have reached a worldwide audience. Pratt's other bestsellers in hardcover and paperback also include:

- Ticket Home
- Paradise Bay
- DAD, The Man Who Lied to Save the Planet
- MOM, The Woman Who Made Oatmeal Stick to My Ribs

The Christ Report, along with his latest work of inspirational fiction released in Spring 2008, As a Man Thinketh…In His Heart, take readers by the hand into a world of possibilities where faith blends with answers to some of life's most perplexing questions about meaning and what matters most.

James and his wife Jeanne have been married thirty years. He is a partner in a company, PowerThink, LLC, devoted to inspiration and self-improvement. For more about his life and writings please visit: www.powerthink.com and his personal website, www.jmpratt.com.

Magical, Mysterious, and Inspirational!!!!!
— Cheryl Metz, Librarian

Franklin-Covey Co-Founder & Co-Chairman, Hyrum Smith

AS A MAN THINKETH…In His Heart is a fascinating continuation of the ideas set forth in James Allen's classic bestseller, *As a Man Thinketh*. Adding to it the principles of heart-powered thinking, Mr. Pratt offers life changing secrets for the 21ˢᵗ century. He does it in such a way that the reader is greatly entertained while pondering the power of thought and its relationship to the heart. Whoever reads this will be infused with not only the desire to change for the better, but the belief that positive change is possible."

❧❦

"I cried, I laughed, I thought, I pondered, I loved more… Thank you so much for sharing this story with me."
— Patricia Sheranian, Businesswoman

❧❦

"What an awesome story! My attention was riveted to the story so much that I couldn't put it down. Another one of my favorite books is Og Mandino's *The Greatest Salesman in the World*. Your book reminded me of his when I finished. Your story has already begun to change me. Thanks for the opportunity to read this novel!
— Lance Andrewsen, Businessman

❧❦

"A highly memorable read! The current challenge between our hearts and minds in this demanding high-tech world is explicit in James Pratt's insightful words, encouraging a fuller utilization of our time in seeking God's grace."
— Howie Beach, Retired, Veteran World War Two

Mary Jean Bentley, Actress, Songwriter, Film & Music Producer

WOW! James, AS A MAN THINKETH... *In His Heart,* is BRILLIANT! Everyone who cares about the human spirit and progressing in a positive way should read your book! I laughed, I cried, and will read it again and again. I will recommend it to all my friends and associates. Congratulations James, on another winner!"

❧❧

This is your best book since *THE LAST VALENTINE!* I loved all the others, but this is just really magical! My husband wouldn't put it down last night until he finished it. We both enjoyed the wonderful love stories woven into it. I'm telling our book club and all our friends that they must read it! A touching, thoughtful, and entertaining story!"
— *Janean and John Hendrickson, City Manager*

❧❧

I LOVE THE BOOK!!!! With love, mystery, going time back, the ghost-writer... Thank you Mr. Pratt for writing it! When will Hampton of Devon come out?
— *Barbara Siniscalchi*

❧❧

Except for Og Mandino, I haven't read fiction authors in many years; and so I was surprised when I picked up, **As a Man Thinketh...** *In His Heart* and couldn't put it down. Once I started, I read for two straight hours. This is Og Mandino at his best! I will be recommending your book to everyone I know.
— *Carlos Packard, CEO, Packard Technologies.*

❧❧

Without a doubt, **As a Man Thinketh...** *In His Heart* offers the success secrets for our fast paced 21st Century! James Allen's 20th Century formula for the inspired and abundant life has just been turbo charged by James Michael Pratt! I highly recommend this book to any serious seeker of self-improvement."
— *James W. Ritchie, Trainer, Speaker, Businessman.*

FREE OFFER

E-Book and Audio Downloads

James Allen's 1902

As A Man Thinketh

Read by New York Times Bestselling Author
James Michael Pratt

E-Book for your Computer or Handheld is the
BONUS BOOK as also found within these pages.

🌐 http://www.powerthink.com/aamt-reg.php